The Game

Winning Moves for the Male New Hire in Corporate America

Kim Beamon

4147-BEAM

To order additional copies of this book, contact:
Xlibris Corporation
1-888-7-XLIBRIS
www.Xlibris.com
Orders@Xlibris.com

Contents

Forward Foreword

When I thought about the people I could ask to write the foreword to my book, big names like Kobe Bryant, Michael Jordan, and a few CEO's came to mind. I thought, "Yeah, people will listen to those guys!" Then I thought, maybe something simpler is needed here. I kept hearing the word "foreword." Foreword. Yeah. *Forward*. So, this foreword (preface) is about *going forward* (onward, toward the future). From time to time, we all need a little inspiration to keep us moving and in the game. With that in mind, I've selected some quotes from some people who, despite whatever odds, did their best. So, be inspired, and go forward!

"It takes deep commitment to change and an even deeper commitment to grow."
Ralph Ellison (1914-1994), writer

"The one thing grander than the sea is the sky. The one thing greater than the sky is the spirit of the human being."
Anonymous

"If your brain can move your body with a split second command thought, imagine what it can do with concentrated and directed thought."
Dr. Therman Evans, physician

"I've had so many downs that I knew the law of averages would be in my favor one day."
Doug Williams, head football coach, Grambling University

"Many times during auditions, I was told that I couldn't carry a note with a bucket, and that I sure couldn't play the piano."
Ray Charles, singer, pianist and composer

"We must not become discouraged."
Booker T. Washington (1856-1915), former slave, educator, adviser to Presidents Theodore Roosevelt and William H. Taft, and founder of Tuskegee Institute

"You can map out a fight plan or a life plan, but when the action starts, it may not go the way you planned, and you're down to your reflexes—which means your training."
Joe Frazier, professional boxer, inducted into the International Boxing Hall of Fame, 1990

"I had to practically hypnotize myself into thinking I was going to be a success."
John Singleton, screenwriter and filmmaker, youngest person and first African American nominated for Best Director Academy Award, 1992

"Emotion is what makes me what I am today. It makes me play bigger than I am."
Charles Barkley, former professional basketball player, NBA and 1992 MVP

√ "The ship's captain cannot see his destination for fully 99 percent of his journey—but he knows what it is, where it is, and that he will reach it if he keeps doing certain things a certain way."
Dennis Kimbro, author and director of Clark Atlanta University Center for Entrepreneurship

"People will know you're serious when you produce."
Muhammad Ali, 10-time world heavy-weight boxing champion

"Change has always been led by those whose spirits were bigger than their circumstances."
Jesse L. Jackson, founder, Rainbow PUSH Action Network

"I'm very sure of myself . . . I know I'm someone special . . . The only limits on me are the ones I put on myself. I am in control of my thinking."
John Raye, founder and president, The Majestic Eagles business development organization

"No one has more confidence in me than I have in myself."
Allen Iverson, professional basketball player, NBA

"If I had to single out one element in my life that has made a difference for me, it would be a passion to compete."
Sam Walton, author and founder of Wal-Mart

"Your creative ability is developed by competition because when you compete, you have to outthink the opposition."
Edward G. Gardner, founder, co-chair of the board of Soft Sheen hair care products

"Facing the rising sun of our new day begun, Let us march on till victory is won."
James Weldon Johnson (1871–1938), lawyer, lyricist, writer, social activist, and first African-American admitted to the Florida bar, 1897

"Knowledge can be obtained (even) under difficulties."
Frederick Douglass (1817-1895), former slave, co-founder and co-editor of *The North Star* newspaper, abolitionist, orator, author, and advisor to President Abraham Lincoln, U.S. Consul to Haiti

"God gave me strength
And it don't make sense
Not to keep on pushing"
Curtis Mayfield (1942-2000), singer, songwriter, and producer

"We give players everything to help them be successful today. . . . We provide everything except heart, desire and competitiveness. That you can't give a player."
Elgin Baylor, former professional basketball player, NBA, named one of the fifty greatest players in the history of the NBA

"Heart can take you far. If you don't have it, you don't have a chance."
Dennis Rodman, former professional basketball player, NBA

Introduction

The *Sport* of Business?!*

Working in corporate America is like surviving in the world of sports. Whatever goals you set, whatever tangible or intangible rewards you seek, whatever is outlined for you to achieve, there are things to *win* from the work you do. You're *competing* against yourself or others. The work group is your *team*, the co-workers your *teammates*. Those who do what you do play the same *position*. The managers are *coaches* and they strategize by holding *team meetings*. The success of your job calls for a *game plan*. And the work year is typically divided into *quarters*.

An Athlete *at Work?!*

Because of the connection between the world of sports and the world of corporate culture, the moment you set foot in the workplace you become what I call a business athlete. The analogy of being an athlete at work can help you to see how you can approach the workplace like a game and play by the rules as you would in any game, using the same skills you probably already possess—those of a good sportsman.

First: As a new hire, *realize* you are a business athlete. As a business athlete, it's important to recognize that at work you're actually in a game. Part of knowing you're in a game is accepting personal responsibility for the position you play. Knowing this automatically lifts you above the attitude of just being happy to have a job—you're there to *play*. Knowing you're in a game also means you are aware that other new hires are trying to create their own success as well—nothing personal, they're just playing the game too. "Game awareness" for the new hire also means, as in any sport, you anticipate all types of opposition within the workplace and even on your team. That you take seriously the constant personal preparation required to out-battle opponents— whether someone's trying to block your moves to improve his position, whether someone perceives you as a threat to his position, or whether it's someone who's simply trying to win some of the same things you are.

Second: *Understand* that for the new hire there is a specific set of rules (written and unwritten). Understand that you may not like the rules, you may not agree with the rules, you may not feel the rules are fair. But if you're going to play the business game, you've got to accept the new-hire rules. Allow this understanding to open your mind. And then both actively and subconsciously identify what the rules are. Watch, listen and strategize to maximize your play within those rules. Third: Make a commitment to *follow the rules*—that is, if you want to compete and not be thrown out (fired) or sit the bench (waste unused potential). Finally, *use the rules* to build the perception you need to make it in corporate America—*play to win*.

But Look, I Made the Team . . .

Many of you enter the workplace holding the right qualifications, the right skills, and the right connections, but needing a better understanding of the new-hire game you're playing and the rules to follow. You may have a college degree, perhaps more than one, or are working toward one. That's a good start. But for that start to unfold into success, you'll have to not only be qualified but do the right things. You must connect your role as a new hire with the rules to follow, so that you'll be behaving in such a way as to be considered professional, successful and intelligent— so that your behaviors reflect you as a team player and a leader. If these things aren't happening, you may fall short of your true potential in the workplace. This is where understanding the game, knowing the new-hire rules, and playing by them gives you the added edge to win.

More Than You Think You Need to Be

Being a success at work is about knowing how to conduct yourself in the workplace (knowing the rules) and then acting on that knowledge (following the rules). Being a success at work also means understanding the power of perception. Knowing and following the new-hire rules is key to building the perceptions of success you need to win. The fact is, as a new hire you must be aware of and responsible for the perceptions you're creating in others. You must realize the connection between what you're saying and doing and the perception that's resulting from what you're saying and doing. Perception is understanding that is based not on thoughtful reflection but on what is seen, heard, observed, or otherwise detected. As a new hire at the office you desire to be seen and heard, yet there are certain things to do and others not to do if you are to have a good chance of being seen and heard in a way that lets you move forward with your skills. As a new hire you must realize that people are watching your actions and, based on what they see and hear, creating a picture of who they perceive you to be.

Perception *is* Reality

Although we are living in a new millennium and today's workplace seems to be more relaxed than ever, there is a set of business rules that remains scarcely changed. If followed, as a new hire these rules will move you towards a professional perception that will work with you instead of against you. This perception will help ensure that you are positioned for the chance to rise to the peak of your potential with little delay. New millennium or not, you've got to understand the fundamentals and make the right moves.

In many cases, your behavior will even be measured against perceptions people may have formed before getting to know you. This may be a surprise to you, but realize that before you say or do a single thing, as a new hire you may be perceived in the following ways: You don't want to work. You're looking for easy ways out. You don't want to follow the rules, or do what you're told. You're looking to do as little as you can. You're money hungry but don't want to really work. You're careless. You're more concerned about looking good than working hard. You have to be carefully watched and monitored. You don't really know what you're talking about. You have little to no power. You're not to be trusted. You're afraid to ask for help. And the list can go on.

Knowing that you may be up against such previously set perceptions, you can see why you must pay attention to the things you say and do. You've got to ensure that your behaviors reflect the person you are: intelligent, skilled, valuable, manageable, teachable, flexible, professional. A team player. A hard worker. Model the right behaviors—do those things you need to do to be perceived positively.

On Point

How do I know what I'm talking about? Good question. For starters, I've been a professional salesperson for over ten years. Having graduated college, I began my sales career as a territory sales representative for the Xerox Corporation. I am currently a National Account Manager at Bell Atlantic Mobile, newly named Verizon Wireless.

So Where Did You Get Your Game?

Day one in corporate America I was well intentioned, highly skilled, competent, and talented. However, there was a time when I made the same mistakes over and over again—painful mistakes, big and small. I had the typical new-hire profile companies looked for in 1988: I was young, black, female, and full of potential. The general assumption from my hiring manager was that I would "do well." After all, I graduated at the top of my college class, I interviewed well, and basically, I had the intelligence and skills they wanted. I was in.

So Far, So Good . . .

I was ready. I started off doing what I knew how to do. But then, the workplace got strange. A feeling came over me that there were certain things I not only didn't know, but clearly was not doing. It was as if there were unspoken rules. And no one was telling me about either the rules or the game. What do I mean? My office teammates constantly talked about our manager behind her back. They accused her of not knowing what she was doing, of being a poor manager and everything else besides. They promised to confront her on some issues they didn't agree with. And of course, I felt the same way, so I chimed in too. But as mysterious as it seemed to me, in team meetings they'd verbally support everything our manager said. So one day I decided they just needed a spokesperson, and I'd be the one to remind them of what we all wanted to say. New hire that I was, I spoke up. Guess what happened? They didn't support the truth I was speaking, the truth that challenged her authority, that same truth we had all agreed on when she wasn't around.

Set up. Fell. Right there in front of everyone, I made the wrong move. I had failed to learn the rules and the game. As a new hire I had failed to recognize this rule: Support the boss. At that moment part of the game was to be a team player. The right move for that play was to support my boss, even if that meant remaining silent, even if I questioned her decision or had a better recommendation. Though my observations about my boss's lack of abilities in certain areas may have been accurate, the issue before her was that I was not being supportive and a team player. As a new hire I shouldn't have brought into question my ability to be a team player by acting as if I was not going to do what the boss decided was best. I needed to say and do the things that would have shown her I was a team player. My critical comments made me look bad. My moves (my actions, my talk) made it difficult for those present to perceive me in any other way than as one who was *not* a team player.

This Talk Wasn't Cheap

As a new hire there were many more rules I didn't follow and many poor perceptions I created. I didn't receive the honors my teammates did: I wasn't selected "Salesperson of the Month," I wasn't asked to lead focus groups. My behavior was preventing me from gaining the type of exposure I knew I was skilled enough to receive. And although I survived violating many of the new-hire rules, I paid a price. I lost out on opportunities to work choice territories (losing chances to make big dollars). I missed the chance to work on the leading sales teams and gain the extra recognition that came with that. I became poorly perceived—everything from being unmanageable to being a liability to the company.

Ouch!

Fortunately, the habit of breaking rules and problems of perception are things that can be turned around. In fact, once I made up my mind, I did what I had to in order to change people's perception of me back to match the person I knew I really was. It was not easy. While I was promoted, let's just say I had a lot of "Come to Jesus meetings" with managers I had spoken ill of. I would later interview with them for a position on their team. And before I could move up, I had to own up to the things I'd said and done. The time I used explaining where I went wrong could have been used making more money and becoming an expert at what I did.

For You—Fundamentally Speaking . . .

As a new-hire business athlete, you must establish control of your game early. Reading this book will help you recognize what to do, how to say and do things to win at the game you're playing. This book will show you where to adjust your level of play and help you create solid moves to get in the paint or above the rim for easy points of perception building at work. It will also help you avoid some common new-hire mistakes. *The Game—Win-*

ning Moves For The Male New Hire in Corporate America serves to assist you in the game *at work*—saying and doing the things that yield winning stats. This book is a game plan that covers your mental and professional approach to work, business attire, work habits, relationship building, work performance, professional and social etiquette, business communications, continuous learning, and your long-term professional goals. The book challenges you to make careful choices about almost every aspect of work life that could affect the way you are perceived—from the amount of cologne to wear to being prepared to move to another position. To add to your ability to win at work, the book points you in the right direction, reminds you of your goals, encourages you, corrects you, motivates you, and helps you see what you might otherwise overlook while you're in the game. Think of it as your "new hire rule book," one that can show you the rules of the game, help you play by the rules and help you use those rules to establish the perceptions you need to move to the next level of promotion.

The Net?

Who is *The Game* written to assist? This book is for you if you are:

- A new hire in your first 12 to 24 months on the job.
- An intern seeking permanent employment.
- A person who's been on the job but who suspects he's not doing something quite right—that *something* is keeping you from deserved promotions or recognition.
- Someone who feels he needs an edge.

To help you focus on the game aspect of business, you're treated as if you're a professional basketball player going into his rookie season. You'll go through pre-season, first and second quarter, halftime, third and fourth quarter, an off-season, and the season will close with business advice. The chapter format is simple: business rules followed by an explanation, and a random mixture of anecdotes and sports analogies ("Sports Talk"). Sports Talk is meant to draw comparisons to similar rules or principles in the game of basketball.

Throughout the book, solely for simplicity's sake, when referring to bosses or co-workers, and in examples or anecdotes, the word "he" will be used—unless we're discussing male and female issues in particular. Be very clear about the fact that you can and will have female bosses and co-workers.

Finally:

The Game will:

- Help you see that certain rules do exist
- Define the new hire's unwritten rules
- Explain the significance and consequences to rule-following
- Offer practical strategies for rule-following
- Share recovery strategies to rule-breaking
- Provide methods to track your progress
- Help you create your own playbook of success.

Remember: *everything* counts. Be encouraged. Be on-purpose. Get your feet set and get ready to shoot the ball!

Pre-Season, Part 1 | Before You Start, Stop

This list serves as a reminder of how well you did to prepare for the job and for the workplace. Before going further, take a moment to glance over the list. Put a checkmark by those things you've completed.

You've . . .

_____ *Decided the position you want.*

_____ *Researched the industry.*

_____ *Identified an industry and personality match.*

_____ *Assessed your personality and abilities.*

_____ *Identified a company and personality match.*

_____ *Selected and researched a corporation.*

_____ *Studied the corporate culture.*

If there are items you haven't completed (even though you may be working already), find the time to address them before too much time passes. Appendix 1 will be helpful in explaining the "how's" and "why's."

My Personal Notes

Take a few minutes and make note of any information that stood out:

_____

_____

_____

_____

_____

_____

_____

_____

What will you do differently as a result of what you've read?

_____

_____

_____

_____

_____

_____

_____

_____

Pre-Season, Part 2 | Before You Begin, Think

As a business athlete you need a trainer. So the next few pages will serve to condition your mind so that your body does what it's supposed to.

Lift each business rule in order to develop and strengthen your "inside stuff"—the stuff you're made of, mentally and emotionally. You'll gain inner personal strength, so that what you're strengthening on the inside will be reflected on the outside.

Inside Stuff

Check it at the Door
Don't bring an attitude to work.

There's nothing more unprofessional than having a nonchalant, lackadaisical, unconcerned, I-don't-care, I-don't-want-to-work-for-nobody-else attitude. Aside from the profit you can help bring to the overall business, understand that your attitude, motivation, quality of work, teamwork, and fulfilled responsibility are also returns on the company's investment in you. Working where you do also brings advantages to your own life, conveniences that you might not have obtained on your own. So show respect for the company and have a good attitude at work. And whatever you do, no matter how bored you may be, no matter how quickly you complete your assignments, no matter who's getting on your nerves, do *not* lay your head down on the desk and take a nap on company time! Even if you're on your break, this is not acceptable.

Your "Will" *Will* Be Done
Commit that you <u>will</u> compete.

Since you're entering the game by your own choice, make up your mind to play. Contend. Strive. Cope. Expect and accept the whole of what it means to compete. You don't quit. You play. You figure out ways to win. Challenges may cause you to pause, but they should also energize and motivate you to climb higher in order to see another way to win.

Strengthen your mind, daily.
Believe.
Trust that all things are possible.

Accept as true that you are capable.

Rely on the fact that you are a professional.

Possess excitement. Contaminate others with a positive attitude.

Remain motivated.

Be convinced of your abilities to overcome challenges.

Know that obstacles are key to discovering your talents.

Embrace change—you will be highly valued if you are flexible.

> *Sports Talk—Get in the game. Play ball. Once the game is on you'll make adjustments. You may decide to take outside shots instead of driving down the lane. Whatever you do, maintain your mental focus. Relax. Keep your composure. Don't pick up a foul. Being ejected isn't worth it. Simply start thinking of ways to outwork the next guy.*

Mushy, Gooey

Know who you are.

Know what you like and dislike. Know what you will tolerate and what you will not. Know your boundaries. Understand your strengths and weaknesses (*I know, nowadays we're not supposed to call weaknesses, "weaknesses." Okay—so how about this: Understand your personal areas of strength and "areas to improve"*). Confront any internal, emotional issues. We all have them, but not all of us deal with them so that they don't manage us or our decisions.

Help is On the Way

Be open to personal development and growth.

If your self-esteem could use a lift, get the assistance you need—motivational books, tapes or even attend a seminar or two.

Is This O.K.?

Resolve personal "needs."

If you tend to look for approval from others, you may need to change your approach and look outside of work to meet those needs. Needing your ideas approved of or needing everyone to like you or affirm you sets you up for a roller coaster ride. If you're more concerned with being liked, you will find you are at other people's disposal—not a good place to be. Whatever method you choose, address issues like these outside the workplace and work diligently to fix them. Behaving inappropriately because of personal issues is draining to you and to those around you, especially when conducting business is the priority.

It's Not Over Until It's Over

Never give up.

Ah, yes, I should tell you about my friend Ricky. Ricky set his mind on becoming a doctor. Ricky graduated college, but failed to make his premed mark to get into medical school. Unlike his doctor-hopeful classmates, he didn't get into medical school the first or second time. But . . . Ricky spent a year searching for another way. Finally, he discovered a slower paced pre-medical program that would potentially accept his test scores. He didn't give up on his dreams to be a doctor, despite the fact that he didn't get a spot on the list to be considered. Instead, Ricky networked with the school's professors and admissions directors, with community doctors, and basically with anyone who could influence his acceptance into the program. Persistence had its way. Ricky was in. Five-year program though it was, with student loans and campus work-study, and despite being the brunt of classmates' jokes, the bottom line is that now, ten years later Ricky is practicing internal medicine. Never give up. Let me repeat: Never give up.

Sports Talk—If you take a shot that doesn't even draw iron, stay with it. Get back on defense, make a good play down the court, and get back into position to take another shot. Don't dwell on the air ball you shot ten minutes ago. If you keep moving and don't mentally check out of the game, you'll have many more chances.

Bench Warming, Are You?
Accept your position on the team.

Okay—so you've accepted your position but you have a suspicion you're being required to do things that you think are beneath your skills. Fret not. Realize that dues cost something. Pay the price. Employers want to know that you'll out-perform regardless of the task. Don't worry, at this point the corporate ladder is a mere footstool. Paying dues gives you the opportunity to learn everything you can. Remember: you are to add value to your position. Be prepared to give a little extra. Bring everything you have to the role.

Hello, Anyone Home?
Pay attention and listen.

Prepare yourself for the meetings you'll attend. Prepare yourself to bring a positive energy to the room. Sit up straight. Have pen and paper. Wear a pleasant smile and look like you're eager to learn. A key element to learning and effective communication is listening. Listening is not talking, debating, challenging, pushing your ideas and recommendations forward or proving how much you know. Listening is not waiting for your turn to talk. Listening is remaining quiet in your mind. It's making careful observations about what you're hearing—what's being said and what's not being said.

Listening is paying attention to the behaviors and expressions of others in the room. Listening is making mental notes (not judgements or comparisons). As a new hire you want to master listening techniques first and foremost so you can learn. Though you are intelligent, it's important not to come across as a know-it-all, someone who is convinced he knows more after the first few days on the job than his tenured teammates. A good listener is often more valued than a good talker. Listening also allows you to hear key business issues, protocol (how things are done and through whom) and analyze how you can add value. This will come in handy later when you're actually asked for professional recommendations.

> ***Sports Talk***—*"Hey rookie, can you handle sittin' pine?" You might have to spend time proving yourself right where you are—on the bench. You may out-perform the starting five during practice, but you may need to wait for your opportunity to get in the game. It's also important not to whine about not getting enough playing time. While you're paying your dues, plan your own strategy for future contributions.*

Goalie, Listen Up
Set goals.

Simply put, a goal is something you want to accomplish. Most goals require time and planning. Goals can be ever evolving and shaped by all kinds of circumstances and experiences. Nevertheless, goals are good to have. Keep thinking about what yours are. You'll even discover that having goals gives you added tolerance to deal with the unexpected curves in your life's path. Funny how you'll keep driving when you know your destination is just around the bend.

Set goals based on your values. Write them down. Prioritize them. Then plot the steps to reach your target. Set realistic time frames in which to accomplish them. Keep your plan handy. Status-check them to see that you're on track. If you're off track, re-group and get back on. Tracking keeps you excited about the steps. It's no accident that, like ladders, goals have steps.

For an exercise in goal setting, see Appendix 2. For encouragement, refer to Appendix 3.

Sports Talk—To be the league's leading three-point shooter, continue to work on your overall game, but before and after practice, spend extra time in the gym shooting three-pointers too.

"If You Don't Get It, You *Don't* Get It!"
Stay informed.

Keeping current is important. If possible, start receiving *The New York Times*, *The Wall Street Journal*, or *USA Today*. Business journals are also excellent ways to stay informed. Read magazines such as *Fortune, Business Week, Forbes*, and *Smart Money*, and depending upon your field, subscribe to industry-specific magazines as well. One way to be perceived as an outstanding team player is to be knowledgeable. The goal is to be the one who first announces the big news of the day. The goal is to be perceived as an expert in your industry, knowing what's going on, who's doing what, big wins, major losses.

Being perceived as knowledgeable makes you powerful. After a while, your teammates will be asking you what's going on with such and such. Your boss might even give you a portion of the team meeting to provide updates. Stay current. You don't have to say a lot or talk about too many news-breaking stories. Interject a headline or two and wait to be asked for the in-depth explanation. Quote your source and summarize.

Sports Talk—Study the moves of the superstars. Find out what they practice. Adapt their ideas with your own creativity. Plan on being the next superstar. Take the time to study the moves of your teammates, as well as your competitors. Study the game tapes, watch the films, and figure out what's going on and how you plan to compete.

Who Really Cares What They Think?
Remember that perception is definitely everything.

So who cares? You do. Perception is reality. *Now that was easy, wasn't it?*

Put on Your Game Face
Decide how you want to be perceived.

Jeff consistently greets others in his office with a cheerful "hello" or "good morning." When he finds his office mates complaining, he helps them consider the brighter side of their problem. Jeff is perceived as a positive, up-beat employee.

Frank regularly converses with his cube-mates and his boss regarding what they did over the weekend. Frank remembers to ask about upcoming birthdays and special events. Frank is perceived as sincere and concerned about others.

You might ask, "What does being nice and speaking to people this way get me?" Glad you asked. If you are perceived as consistently positive and upbeat, it says that the stresses of the job don't affect you negatively. You're seen as constant and steady. And when people must make decisions about which job you might do well in or fail this perception helps you because decisions are often based on your ability to not get stressed out by the challenges. The perception that you are concerned suggests that while you are business minded, you have the ability to relate to people— a good management quality. When it comes to your attitude, it's important to choose behaviors that will make you look good.

These behaviors—complaining about how bad the system is; acting frustrated (huffing and puffing) and reminding your boss how inadequate everything is—will work *against* the professional perception you want. Yet what will work *with* the perception you're trying to create is acknowledging issues as challenges and asking questions like, "What if we tried it this way? Do you believe that would help?" Or, "What might work is if we considered going at it like this. Would you like me to try?"

> **Sports Talk**—*Team Leader: When your team is down, lead the pep talk. Positive Motivator: When a guy takes a bad shot, be the first one to run over and encourage him to shake it off and keep shooting.*

Time Out!

On the following page, decide a couple of ways you want to be perceived (i.e., as timely, helpful, willing), set the goals, and chart the steps to get there.

How Do I Want To Be Perceived?

Goal #1: _____

By When? _____

What do you need to do to accomplish this goal?

1.   By When? _____
2.   By When? _____
3.   By When? _____
4.   By When? _____
5.   By When? _____

Goal #2: _____

By When? _____

What do you need to do to accomplish this goal?

1.   By When? _____
2.   By When? _____
3.   By When? _____
4.   By When? _____
5.   By When? _____

For additional perception goal setting samples, see Appendix 4.

My Personal Notes

Take a few minutes and make note of any information that stood out:

_____

_____

_____

_____

_____

_____

_____

_____

What will you do differently as a result of what you've read?

_____

_____

_____

_____

_____

_____

_____

_____

Pre-Season, Part 3 | Before You Leave the House, Look in the Mirror and Check the Closet

And if there's inside stuff, you know there's "outside stuff." The next part of pre-season gets you in gear from the outside. Business athlete, once you're thinking clearly, you'll be ready to get cleaned up and dressed for the game.

Along with thinking right, you must make a radical decision to look and even smell right.

Pre-Season ends with a list of helpful tools to ensure you'll be professional and productive. Finish this section and you'll find yourself at center court waiting for the light show and the announcer to call your name.

Outside Stuff

The Shower Scene

Keep your body clean.

I'm assuming we all know we must wash before work, right? I know I don't even have to go there. *Just checking to make sure you're still with me.*

Think of the body products you might use before getting dressed: soap, deodorant, body lotion, cologne. What you smell like is significant. Put on a small amount of cologne. You don't want people to know you've been down the hall long after you've left the building. If you're using bar soap and you plan to wear cologne, use fragrance-free soap and fragrance-free body lotion. And remember to splash or spray your cologne *before* putting on your shirt.

Right Guard and *Wet Stains*?—Sweating is not something you can always control. If you tend to sweat through your shirt, regardless of the temperature, try to find a brand of deodorant to help reduce the amount of sweating you do. As much as possible, wear white shirts that don't show the sweat as much. If you can, try to keep your jacket on. Otherwise, refrain from lifting your arms behind your neck. It may be helpful, for the same reason, to wear dark colored shirts. If you have a truly serious sweating tendency, consider changing shirts mid-way through the day, or at least the undershirt, especially if your body gives off an odor with the sweat. And when the underarm of the shirt has turned yellow cease wearing it to work.

Wash Your Mouth Out With Soap
Keep your breath fresh.

Keep your teeth brushed and your mouth fresh and clean. After each meal floss (in private) and clean any food particles out of your teeth. White teeth and fresh breath really add to your image in ways I don't have the words for. (*I trust you know what I mean*). Consider brushing your teeth after lunch. Keep a limitless supply of breath mints handy. Be prepared to have fresh breath at all times, especially if you're a coffee drinker or smoker or tend to eat foods that carry heavy odors. If you have problem teeth, you might consider paying to have them corrected (braces, bleaching, etc.).

A Hairy Situation
Keep your hair professionally styled and clean.

At this point in your career, wearing anything other than a conservative hairstyle can be tricky. I'm not saying dreads, bleached hair, braids or afros are totally unacceptable, just that they speak words about who you are and what you believe. Words that may not work for you and the professional image you're trying to create—words you can't be sure everyone in corporate America will understand right now.

Wash your hair well enough that it doesn't smell old. Comb or brush your hair before putting on your shirt and suit jacket. No matter how dandruff-free your hair is, take a moment to wipe your shoulders, neck, and back. If you dye your hair, avoid dramatic colors (*I think you know what I'm talking about*) which would draw attention and curiosity.

Keep your face clean and, to be on the safe side, closely shaven, avoiding facial hair (mustache, beard, side-burns). Remove unsightly nose hairs, and if you have totally unruly eyebrows consider having them shaped by a stylist.

Oil Change
Keep dry skin moist.

Moisturize the primary parts of your body that people will see—the face, the hands, and the lips. Be extra sure to keep your hands moisturized, especially in the winter.

Nailed Down—No long nails! Nails should not be longer than the tip of your finger. Make sure you clean the dirt from under your nails, something that definitely needs attention if you have messy hobbies. If you have hard-to-handle nails, consider professional manicures.

To Clean or Not to Clean
Keep your clothes clean.

Suits, shirts, and ties need to be dry cleaned on an as-needed basis—shirts more frequently than suits and ties. Periodically wash your shirts by hand to soak any dry-cleaning odors out of them.

Pointing Out the Obvious
Accept the reality that what you wear counts—really.

Before you buy a book, you look at the cover and decide if it looks like it's worth your money. What people see you wearing is often how people see *you*. Dress-for-success experts say professional dress doesn't necessarily guarantee success, but dressing poorly almost always guarantees failure. What I know from experience is this: Your appearance at work counts, all day, every day. Have these things in mind when dressing: Be clean. Be conservative.

***Sports Talk**—Get dressed for the game you're playing. You wouldn't wear a football helmet, shoulder pads and cleats on a basketball court, now would you? You wouldn't wear street shoes on the basketball court either—wearing anything other than basketball shoes during the game would be simply unprofessional.*

Professionally Speaking

Focus on looking professional rather than fashionable.

Remember to dress for the future position you want. If you're interested in an upper-management or director-level position, start dressing the part now. The traditional look that seems to be most favored consists of a fine-quality gray or navy suit, white straight-collar shirt, with optional French cuffs, worn with dark socks and expensive, thin-soled leather shoes. The distinctive signature is said to be the tie (usually a designer label like Chanel or Brioni). In any case, choose ties that show a nice contrast and avoid tie designs that are outdated. Keep in mind how a suit is going to add to the perception you desire. Avoid suits that are snug or tight—pants and sleeves too short. Wear crisp shirts, starched and ironed at the cleaners. If ready-made suits don't fit properly, you might consider having your suits made-to-measure or personalized to fit your particular body measurements.

The Details . . .

* Suits—have six to eight. Solids and Pinstripes—medium shade of navy, navy pinstripe or chalk stripe, medium shade of gray, gray multicolor stripe, medium shade of olive, medium shade of taupe or tan. Plaids—black or navy subtle plaid, black or white nailhead. Houndstooth—black and white.
* Shirts—have ten long-sleeved business shirts—seven white, two blue, one burgundy stripe.
* Shoes—have three pair (a pair of black cap-toe, black tassel loafers, and cordovan slip-ons). Each pair will need a pair of cedar shoetrees.
* Socks—have ten pair (dark colors only).
* Belts—have two (black or brown).
* Ties—have twelve to eighteen (assorted colors to coordinate with suits).

★ Accessories—avoid too much jewelry. Big link gold bracelets, gold chains and multiple rings on each hand may be better left for your weekend social time. To maintain a conservative appearance, keep your look simple: a nice watch and one ring per hand.

Other Stuff to Think About—Some general advice given by the experts:

Thin men should avoid stripes that run lengthwise. If you're slender, take advantage of padded shoulders, trousers with cuffs, and horizontal patterns in neckties to add a little width.

Shorter men can look taller by wearing pinstripe suits with single-breasted two-button styling. If you're short, omit cuffs altogether and make sure jacket and sleeve lengths are precise.

Heavy men look flattering in single-breasted or six-to-one double-breasted suits. If you're heavy-set, make sure your jacket is roomy enough to button and always wear it closed. Braces are a plus as well.

Sportin' the Look
Dress appropriately for your chosen field.

Figure out what's considered appropriate in the industry in which you work. For example, in the financial industry, since money is the focus, people want to sense stability and trust from the person they're doing business with. The dress code then, is generally conservative. However, in the advertising field, there may be more breathing room for dressing creatively while still appearing professional. If you're an advertising executive, your client should see you as bold, creative, not afraid to take risks.

This, That, and *The Other* . . .
Dress the way you want people to think of you.

Because there can be so many variables, you have to ask yourself, "What message am I trying to send?" If you're a creative person, working in a creative environment like the entertainment or magazine industry, the dress code tends to allow room for you and your personal one-night-stand with clothes, but don't go pioneering new boundaries, going where no man has gone before.

Read it Over
Go get a dress-for-success book!

The benefit of reading dress for success books is that there are so many elements to consider: what's appropriate, what types of fabrics are acceptable, what's affordable, what's attractive—color and body type. There are the jackets—single-breasted, double-breasted, light colored, dark colored, patterned or single-colored? There are the shirts—cotton, polyester-cotton, wrinkle-resistant, white, pale blue, creams, button-down collar, straight collar, rounded collar. There are the ties—silk, wool, red, black, stripes, dots, solid, patterned, prints, bow. There's the concept of what's considered business attire and business casual. Then there's the task to combine all these pieces together so you look good! *Go get the book!*

A Rookie's Salary
Don't break your bank!

"Now, wait a minute," I can hear some of you saying. " Yeah, right. My money is too funny right now." *What I'll say is, "Well, it's a good thing that you can pretty much get by just fine wearing the same suit without appearing as if you have no money."* But seriously, a few ideas here might generate some extra cash you can put toward building the right wardrobe. Request that all gifts be in the form of cash or department store gift certificates. Save the money you'd spend on other things that can wait, and spend the money on a quality suit for work. All things in perspective, the new car might have to wait. The expensive apartment might have to wait—either that, or get a couple of roommates. The clubbin' and entertainment might have to be put on hold until you meet your new business goals. Keep in mind, you don't have to have everything all at once. But you do need to make the right start at that new job.

T.G.I.C.F.?!*
Don't be overly casual.

Casual Fridays and Dress Down Days are not days when you're free to dress like you're going out to the club or to a baseball game. Casual days are on the rise; companies believe casual wear boosts morale, energy levels, creativity, and productivity. Although the rules aren't crystal clear, I agree with the experts: The casual clothes you wear around the house on weekends are probably not the same casual clothes you'll wear to work.

Confusing Friday—Tons of variables to consider when dressing for Casual Friday—the company you work for, the industry, the geography; whether or not you're going to see a client, whether or not that client is having casual day, whether you're staying in the office, whether your client is coming to see you in your office on casual day; what position you hold, whether you're in sales, marketing, support services, whether you travel across regions. See what I mean? Because there are so many considerations, you'll really be the one to decide. The important thing is to do your research and keep your look professional.

Casual Day in General—Find out whether you're dressing for dress-down day in a style that is truly casual, business casual, mainstream business casual, superb mainstream business casual, baseline casual, or executive business casual. And find out what each category means to the company you work for. Many companies will actually publish a detailed definition of what business casual means to them.

A male professional can still maintain a professional image even though casually dressed, following guidelines that are relatively easy to stay within. Wear nicely pressed blue, black, or brown trouser-cut cotton pants, or double-pleated khaki, olive, tan, or taupe cotton twill pants, or slacks. Wear a quality polo shirt or cotton turtleneck, sport coat, and well polished shoes, Hush Puppies, or black or brown suede shoes, and of course, be fully groomed (clean shaven, hair cut, clean nails, etc.). When in doubt, lean toward the conservative side. If all else fails, and you're still confused, dress the way your boss does. If your boss is of the opposite sex, find her counterpart, someone you feel is safe to emulate.

Tuck in Your Jersey, Check Your Laces, And . . .
Sweat the small stuff.
Check to see that you have a . . .

- Briefcase (or some type of professional carrying case)
- Pen
- Portfolio
- Business card holder
- Calculator
- Map—very helpful for sales positions
- Day-timer/Pocket calendar
- Breath mints

My Personal Notes

Take a few minutes and make note of any information that stood out:

_____

_____

_____

_____

_____

_____

_____

_____

What will you do differently as a result of what you've read?

_____

_____

_____

_____

_____

_____

_____

_____

1Q | Before You Play, Check In

The adrenaline that's flowing from pre-season is what you need for this first quarter. At work, use this period to set the tone for your game, observe your opponents, and slowly lay the foundation for the way you're going to move about and score the points you need to win.

First quarter business rules are your fast breaks, lay-ups, and free throws.

Get in the game—it's time to play!

Tip Off

Early Bird . . .
Arrive early, stay a little late.

Develop the habit of arriving 15-30 minutes before work and leaving 15-30 minutes after you're scheduled to be off. This gives you the perception of being committed and eager to contribute.

"Hello"
Be cordial.

Speak to everyone. Speaking can demonstrate self-confidence and concern for others. These are definitely good ways to be perceived.

Even though you speak, there will be a few who'll stand right next to you at the fax machine and seem not to notice you. They usually have a lot to offer and may well be very successful. Because they're focused on exactly what they're doing at the time, they may forget to speak. Understand: They will remember you for speaking to them. Don't be offended.

On the Count of Three—Say, "Cheese." Smiling is especially key when you're having a challenging day. When people ask how you're doing, even if you have 700 good reasons to complain, respond with something positive. Whatever you do, don't complain—you don't want to be perceived as a whiner. If you start down the complainer's path, stop mid-sentence and recover. You can say, "You know what? Now that I think about it, I'm really doing just fine."

I Get Around
Initialize your work area.

Once you've been hired you'll be shown where you'll be sitting. Don't wait to be shown everything else too. Take the initiative to find out your office number and set up your voicemail. Find out the fax numbers you'll be using. Set up your workstation—get logged on to the computer system, establish your email and make sure your computer is printing documents at the printer near your work area. If need be, sign up for training on the company's computer system and any special programs you'll be working with. Order business cards, if applicable.

You Have Not, Because You Ask Not—Asking for help may be a difficult concept to digest and apply, but—get over it! Ask for what you need. No one is going to take you by the hand and tell you what to do or show you how to do everything. If you're not sure about something, ask. *You* are ultimately responsible for what you learn, no one else.

Home Court Advantage
Get the company provided tools.

Many companies provide as part of your job a company pager, cellular phone, laptop, Palm Pilot, car, gas card, calling card, credit card, and other company provisions. If you receive any of these items for company use, make sure you understand the policies and procedures, liabilities, and limitations (keep a copy of all the documentation you sign and read the documents carefully). Develop a clear understanding about the difference between personal use and company use. Respect company privileges such as the use of local and long distance calling, corporate credit cards, cellular phones, email, and the Internet.

Since You Live in My House, You'll Live by My Rules
Don't abuse what you're given to use.

Phone calls should be 99 percent business related. When

you're in the office, you're there to conduct company business. Personal calls should last no more than several minutes. If such conversations last longer, you need to have those particular conversations away from the office. Avoid whispering on the phone or talking in a low tone of voice, especially if this is not the way you usually talk on the phone.

Personal long distance calls should be made only in the case of an emergency. Most companies have the ability to track all calls, local and long distance. The last thing you want is your boss asking you to explain who lives in California when you live in Detroit. If you have a company calling card, check the policy regarding personal calls and weekend usage.

The same holds true when using the fax machine—incoming and outgoing faxes should be business related, not personal. If you're allowed to play music at your desk, keep the volume at a low level so others in your work area are unable to hear. If your radio is part of a television, resist the urge to *watch* television. Listening to loud music or watching television while at work, even if it's your lunch break, will come across as unprofessional.

The Fine Print—If your job provides you with a cellular phone, limit your incoming and outgoing calls to business. Some companies have a special rate for employee cellular phones. Use that program and make your personal calls from your own personal phone. If you're making personal calls on the company cellular phone, keep them under a minute or two and keep them to one or two a month. Unless permitted, avoid using the cellular phone after work hours or on weekends. A detailed bill can be provided, outlining each call, the number called, the time of the call, the duration of the call, the city the call was made from— need I say more? And even though some cellular services offer voice privacy, I recommend discussing nothing confidential over the phone line (business or personal).

Pass the Information Please . . .
Learn about company resources.

Become an information junkie. Make a habit of reading everything that is made available to you. Peruse the corporate Intranet. All the information you can eat is typically located there. The Intranet usually houses information on most every department represented in the company. If the company has locations in various parts of the U.S., information about those locations will generally be represented as well. You can't go wrong by surfing the corporate Intranet. You'll be able to educate yourself and come across as resourceful. The extra 15 to 30 minutes you have from arriving before and staying after work is also time well spent logging on to the Intranet. If an Intranet site is not available, find a company directory or annual report.

It's On You
Initiate a meeting with your boss.

As quickly as possible, schedule an appointment with your boss to review what will be expected of you over the next 30-60-90 days. In case you're thinking it's your boss's responsibility to "tell you" what he expects, or to come to you to let you know what's up—think again. I'm not saying you won't have a boss who does, but taking initiative will do more for your image than waiting for your boss to tell you he would like to talk to you about your role and his expectations. Also, taking the initiative lets your boss know you're serious about the contribution you're prepared to make. Meet during a time that's best for your boss—early mornings before the day gets started, lunch time (if it's convenient for your boss) or at the close of the day.

You might also take this time to figure out what type of approach is acceptable to your boss. Can you approach the boss the same way your teammates can? Can you use the same approach as a teammate who is of another culture or gender? Can you be assertive without your boss feeling intimidated or that you're out of control? The emphasis is on *you* because depending on your personality and a host of other variables, you might discover that the approach another teammate uses will not be the one that works for you and the boss. At this point, observe and make mental notes. Be prepared to adjust your approach, at least initially. After a period of time and once you've had a chance to build a relationship with your boss you might be able to resume your natural approach.

Realize that clear communication with your boss is going to be key to your success. Remember to include your boss in all your activities—either invite him to participate or at least give him a written summary of the activities you're participating in, whether he asks for the information or not. If a summary of activities form doesn't exist, create one and review it with your boss at the end of each week. Summarizing your activities also allows your boss an opportunity to verify the importance of what you're doing, and to add his thoughts and advice.

The Initial Meeting With Your Boss
You'll want to cover:

- Your job description and pay plan
- Your role on the team
- Expectations and clear objectives
- How to contact your boss
- Empowerment and accountability
- Business goals
- Corporate goals
- Role of your teammates
- Company organizational chart
- Significant policies and procedures
- Your 30-60-90 day Action Plan

Refer to Appendix 5 for details of each element.

How'd You Do That?

Notice what successful habits people practice and emulate them.

Notice what tools your boss and teammates use to be successful. Observe what publications are on their desks. Check out the habits successful co-workers practice, and try a few on for yourself. See if they help you become more effective and productive, and if so, make them your habits.

Two Eyes Are Better Than One

Look, listen and learn.

One of the most valuable ways to learn successful methods is to spend a day working alongside a successful person. This is often referred to as "shadowing." Be sure to let your boss know your plans. Let's say you're a customer service representative. You might want to spend a day with the top customer service rep. Listen in on their calls to see first-hand how they respond to customers. Note the resources they have readily available. Catch the attitude they display. If you have a corporate sales job, ride along with one of the top performers. Observe their selling techniques, objection handling, and closing skills.

From the Observation Deck—You might invite a top performer to share in your day as well. Not only do you gain valuable feedback for improving your skills—you're also creating the perception that you are open to continuous improvement, that you are teachable.

If you're able, spend some time with top performers outside of your department. You'll demonstrate your skills for future assignments, learn to appreciate other aspects of the business, and you'll create the perception that you're interested in more than just one area of the company.

Rules to Eat By

Avoid the "lunch bunch."

If you have specific lunch hours, keep them. If you have

more freedom and flexibility for lunch, make wise decisions about the way to use the time. Avoid the "lunch bunch." The lunch bunch is a group of people who make habits of taking two-hour lunches that include doing a little shopping, getting a haircut or even playing a little golf. The pressure can be great, but the perception you risk is that of goofing off on company time. So you're more in charge of your own time, bring your lunch and eat on or near the premises, or if you need to drive to get lunch, drive your own car. An extended lunch every so often is O.K., just let your boss know your plans, and make sure it's not during the busiest time at work.

A,B,C—1, 2, 3
Develop the habit of being organized.

Not always an easy task—but you'll need to develop good organizational habits. Some general tips:

A—Ask for assistance. If organization is not your strong point, and though the thought of asking for help may not be part of your character or make-up, observe those who are organized. See where they put things, what types of files they use (hanging files, desktop file folder separators, file cabinets) and emulate. Or just simply ask where they keep this and that. You have to develop a system that works for you.

B—Be neat. Keep your desk and work area uncluttered. Even if you feel you work better with six hundred pieces of paper everywhere, at the end of the day, try to remove the mound of clutter. You can pull it back out the next day.

C—Complete the task. In today's work environment, the concept of "multi-tasking" is the latest craze. It's even become an expectation. However, there's a way to multi-task without the endless shuffle of paper. You can file documents in folders and file the folder until you actually need to use the information inside. This way you've done something with the piece of paper. To really be effective at this involves decision-making.

What Am I Saying? You have five pieces of paper on your desk. What do you do? Before you pick up any of the remaining four, complete the task required by the first one. If you have to go back to a piece of paper for reference, file it and go back to it when you need to. Make a note in your planner to follow up on the task until it's complete. When you need to go back to that task, take the piece of paper out of the file. This way, papers don't pile up everywhere. As the task is followed up on, let the paper be read, filed, or thrown away.

The *Ifs* Have It—*If* you need to forward a copy to someone— *copy and forward*. *If* you need to read and file for future reference—*read and file*. *If* you need to respond in writing— *write the memo and send*. *If* you need to follow up by email—*do so*. *If* you need to remind yourself to perform a future activity— *note the information in your day-timer*.

The point is, *whatever* the activity or task, try and complete it before you go on to the next piece of paper, or else you'll end up shuffling the same papers on your desk. If the task cannot be completed in a timely fashion, file the paper and continue to work on the task. Write down the things you need to do. It's much easier to look at a list of things to do in your planner and know where to access the piece of paper, than it is to look at six bazillion pieces of paper all over the place.

1—Use a daily planner.

Whatever device you use—paper planner, electronic planner, slim pocket calendar—plan your week. Before the week gets under way, have your goals for the upcoming week already decided. At the end of each week, check to see what you've actually accomplished. Whatever remains outstanding, record it as a new goal for a different day so you're constantly looking forward, not backward.

This is where a time management class pays off—you'll learn how to prioritize the day's activities in order to reach your goals for the week to meet your goals for the month, and so forth. If you haven't already done so, ask if a time management seminar is available to you. If the company doesn't provide the class, look into taking one on your own time.

2—Develop a practical filing and sub-filing system.

Even if you're an electronic king living in his paperless world—using Palm Pilots or some other digital wizardry with the greatest of ease—you'll still need to know how to file actual hard-copy documents. Proper filing (hard-copy or electronic) is key to staying organized and spending less time trying to find things you remember having just seen . . . *somewhere.*

Don't You Know—I've literally spent days trying to locate documents that I didn't take the time to file. At one point in my career, my idea of filing was to have two or three large stacks of paper on my desk. I separated documents by turning paper the opposite direction of the paper below it. I could always find that one piece of paper with that one bit of information I needed—but looking through the pile with someone on hold seemed to add extra pressure to my job. I was not as productive as I could have been because usually I'd have to ask people to let me call them back after I found the information they needed. In order to keep up with the pace of business, I certainly had to change my ways.

And a note about filing emails. With the abundance of email, you might consider learning how to create electronic file folders to organize important email documents. The same filing principles apply as for paper files.

Typical ways to file customer, company and personal information include filing alphabetically, by dates, by events, by customer names, by products, by promotions, by policies and procedures—the list can go on. Separate customer, company, and personal files.

Customer files contain facts relative to your clients: business cards, annual reports, proposals, letters, customer history, so on and so forth.

Company files may include internal contact names and numbers, policies and procedures, and departmental communications, as well as marketing information—corporate news releases, competitive information, product information. Keeping files for all of this is valuable primarily to have a resource of accurate information to perform your job.

Personal files might include your benefits information, performance appraisal documents and related materials, salary and compensation information, vacation requests, and so on. You should keep this information secure at all times. I even recommend keeping copies at home. I suggest keeping other personal items at home as well—letters and cards from your significant other or anything that reflects your private life beyond perhaps photographs on your desk.

3—Document.

Typically, people in the workplace refer to the process of documenting whenever there's an issue in question about a particular event or course of action. Documenting can have a negative connotation, but it doesn't have to be negative. Documenting simply means keeping a record (usually in written form) of policies, procedures, actions, and words relating to a given situation, decision, or event.

The Procedures Involved—Copying and filing hard or softcopy documents is sometimes referred to as "creating a paper trail." The paper trail could consist of correspondence (memos, emails, handwritten notes) which serves as proof or justifies your action in a given situation.

When Do You Document? If you think an action or decision of yours has the potential to be questioned—or just to cover yourself. I'm not advocating suspicion or paranoia, recording and copying everything people say or do. I am saying that when your gut tells you to save something for future reference, or you have a thought that something might be questioned in the future, this is the time to keep documentation of everything that was said and done by you and by others involved.

Another reason documentation is important is because business moves so fast, people really do forget what they may have said and often rely on someone else to remember. Finally, performance issues and adherence to company policies and procedures are matters that are always worth documenting. Make sure you have proof in a format other than your recollection.

When There's No Evidence—Send emails that need a reply. Print the reply and file. Trade voicemails and save the responses. Many voicemail systems erase saved messages after a period of time, so you'll need to periodically save the messages if you feel you'll need the information. After a meeting, follow up with a letter that summarizes what was said, action items determined, and follow-up dates. Give those involved copies and file. Follow up with an email to confirm receipt and feedback. Print the reply and file.

Hard or soft-copy documents are facts that are difficult to argue against—they build credibility and help eliminate the "he says, she says." Go about documenting in a professional manner. You're not trying to threaten anybody you're just keeping a quiet paper trail in case help is needed to answer a question or two in the future.

Spell That For Me Please
Spell check.

Spell names correctly—clients and co-workers. Rather than

risk unintentionally offending Eddie, it's easier to ask if his name ends with a "y" or an "ie." On all correspondence, use your software's spell-check feature—either the automatic one or the actual dictionary. You'll build the perception that you are conscientious and accurate.

What Do You Think?
Ask experts.

Be selective when taking advice from co-workers who've been on the job less than a year. I'm not saying they have nothing to offer they just may not know how to direct you in ways that serve your best interests.

> **Sports Talk**—*A rookie who sits the bench may be a good shooter, but how well can he direct you when he hasn't been on the court long enough to have played through the various elements of the game? He's unlikely to be able to prepare you for the day you're at the free-throw line shooting a one-and-one—a second to go in regulation, one point down.*

Email's Reality
Respect the use of email.

Email, email, email . . . the simplest idea to remember is *whatever* is typed and sent from your office computer has the potential to be viewed by the company. Even though an email is deleted, almost all email is recorded on the office's system server. Messages sent eons ago may still live on. Companies also have the ability to know where you're sending emails and who's sending you emails. Simply be aware that what you're sending and receiving can be monitored. It's also public knowledge that many business executives randomly read employee email as well as listen in on phone conversations. So far, this is legal.

What? I was just kidding. As a joke, Frank sent several emails that contained profane jokes to a few women in the office. He thought they were funny. But the ladies didn't. In fact, one young lady took the evidence to her boss. Her boss agreed that the emails were inappropriate. Frank never received a verbal warning—his boss figured Frank knew better. Another profane and inappropriate email was sent just to bug the girls one last time. The same young lady went to personnel this time, and within a day Frank was asked to resign. His boss meanwhile, was reassigned to a lower position—it was obvious to management that he wasn't able to run a team allowing that type of behavior.

Tangled Net
Respect the use of the Internet.

It's not that companies forbid surfing. Just be aware that there is software available to companies that allow them to track the sites you visit, how long you visit and see which Internet games you might be playing. Software is available to alert someone in Information Systems every time something's done on the network, especially things that are against corporate policy. And as of now, this type of monitoring is legal. Anything other than business-related sites should be avoided while using the office computer.

True Costs
Respect the expense policy.

If your job involves expensing or being reimbursed for money you spend conducting company business, respect the policy. When filling out expense reports, be honest. If you're expensing a business lunch, be sure you actually took a customer—and not your friends. If you're out of town on business travel, and you have dinner with a friend, if your friend pays his portion or even if you pick up the entire bill, expense only your portion, not the entire bill. If you get reimbursed for mileage, again, be honest. If you only drove 15 miles, put 15 miles, not 35. Remember: the perception you want is that you care about how the company's money is being spent. And, if you are active in your company's profit-sharing program, exaggerating your expenses means you are really wasting your own money.

No, No, No
Avoid discussing your job offer.

Do not discuss your salary, what you were offered, or anything that relates to money with anyone at work. You never know what other people might be making. If it gets out that you earn more or less than your peers, somebody's going to be upset. Your boss won't appreciate the challenge you have just created either.

My Personal Notes

Take a few minutes and make note of any information that stood out:

_____

_____

_____

_____

_____

_____

_____

_____

What will you do differently as a result of what you've read?

_____

_____

_____

_____

_____

_____

_____

2Q | Before You Burn, Stoke Your Fire

Now that you've got your head in the game and you've had time to observe and adjust, it's time to settle in and make your presence known. The second quarter should be spent running well thought-out plays. In this quarter, you'll be shooting primarily three pointers in the area of relationship building.

These points are a little harder to come by and require disciplined focus. Use this time to develop a plan for relationship building with your boss—from there, include others.

At the close of the quarter you'll have an opportunity to score points with your co-workers—building your stat sheet for a successful career.

Could You Tell Me Your Name Again?
Realize relationship building is a must.

Relationship building is a critical element in your success in the workplace. Building relationships takes commitment, time, and perseverance. Consider the elements of a good relationship: trust, concern, honesty, respect. These are the elements you'll be working to build with all the people you work with, especially your boss.

The better these work relationships are, the easier it is to accomplish your business goals. You don't need to rush these relationships though. You may find that certain people seem stiff or indifferent—until you get to know them a little better. What they might be saying is that they value genuine relationships, which take time. This is an area you'll find yourself working on continuously.

A quick note: Over time there may be people you won't especially care for—nevertheless, think of at least one good thing about them (like the fact that they show up for work). When you refer to them, and when someone else asks you what you think about them, challenge yourself to keep your comments positive, no matter what you think.

Who Are You?
Develop a relationship plan with your boss.

Knowing your boss goes further than knowing his name and title. Getting to know your boss takes time as well. Work your way into this relationship, much as you would with someone you were dating: be sincere and start simple.

Slowly find out the answers to the following questions:

About your boss—Where was he born and raised? Where did he go to school (i.e., high school)? What college did he attend? What was his major?

About your boss's family (wife/kids)—Where did they meet? How many kids do they have? What are their names and ages?

What schools do they attend? What activities or hobbies are they involved in?

More about your boss's family (parents/siblings)—Where were they born and raised? Where did his parents go to school? How did they meet? What business are they in? How many brothers and sisters does the boss have? Where do they live? What are they doing?

Over time you'll want to know more about your boss's:

- Career experiences
- Business goals and aspirations
- Hobbies and interests

And . . . of course when the opportunity arises, you'll want to meet the boss's family, perhaps at a company event.

How Is This Helpful? Think back to what it feels like standing in an elevator with people you don't know. What is everybody doing? Looking up at the lighted numbers above the doors, staring straight ahead (unless the elevator has reflective doors!), looking down at their feet—just about anything to occupy themselves until they can break out of that elevator. The point: It's uncomfortable to be around people you don't know. Getting to know your boss makes both of you more comfortable around one another. And, in general, people like to feel that they are interesting, and know that others are concerned for their well being. So it's always nice to ask about your boss's family and to keep in mind those things he likes to do and talk about them from time to time.

The relationship you establish with your boss impacts other areas of your career. When you apply for a position in another department—guess what? Your boss generally approves the move. When you're interviewing for that position, a follow-up conversation with your boss usually takes place. He'll be asked by the hiring manager to comment on you, your behavior, your ability to be a team player, and your overall image. At this point it pays to have built a solid and loyal business relationship with your boss.

Yes or No?
Honesty is still the best policy.

Resist the temptation to hide any part of the truth. Even if your job is on the line, tell the truth. You don't ever want your integrity questioned. If your boss finds out you have not been totally honest (and he will), no matter how you think you explained your way out of it, he will likely have doubts about most everything you say in the future. If the boss can't trust you to tell him the truth, he will not likely trust you with additional responsibility or even a promotion. Honesty makes trust come quicker and easier. Honesty also sustains your own self-respect. *Never mind that being dishonest could cost you your job!*

Just Do It
Keep your boss in the loop.

Keep your boss informed. If he doesn't see you everyday, let him know your work schedule. Let him know about decisions you're making. If you know someone is going to call him, give him a call first to let him know. Keep him from being caught off guard. If you've given his name to someone as a contact, let him know. If you're dealing with a problem situation that could escalate (go above you and him), let him know. Even if you've resolved a crisis or prevented what could have become a disaster, let him know what happened and the steps you took.

When you come up with business solutions, as a courtesy and out of respect, inform your boss. Also ask him for feedback or advice if there's something he wants you to do in addition to carrying out your idea. Depending on the situation, you may even want to let your boss present your ideas—remember to keep copies for your files (for your performance review, which we'll discuss later).

Your goal is to make sure your boss looks good—you're not trying to outshine him at this point, you're trying to build credibility and a trusting, loyal working relationship. Generally, your boss knows when you deserve credit for an idea. If the idea is good, people will ask more questions, your boss will probably ask you for answers, and before you know it, everyone else will know who the idea belonged to. In such a case, not only are you perceived as bright, but politically savvy as well. You won't have to say a word. Remember, even if your boss gets promoted based on your good ideas, there's a good chance he'll see that you move up as well.

Stand By Your Man *(or Woman)*
Protect your boss.

When you're asked how you like your boss or when someone asks your opinion about a decision your boss made—protect him. How you respond is critical—no disparaging comments, no negative feedback, no body language or facial expressions that suggest anything other than support.

Protecting your boss in front of others is more important than being right. Even if your boss has done something that, in your opinion, is really stupid, when asked, your response should not give this opinion away. Try an answer like this: "My boss has a lot of experience in that area, and I am positive things will be just fine." Usually you can walk away or change the subject and talk about something else.

Door #1, #2 or #3
Try not to "open-door" your boss.

To "open-door" someone is to challenge them publicly—in front of at least one other person. Avoid saying or doing anything that could be interpreted as a public challenge—like bad-mouthing a decision he's made during your team meeting.

The time will come when you'll want to ask your boss for clarification or offer an alternative perspective—but try to do this behind closed doors or even away from the office. If you feel passionate about your feedback and you must comment in a group setting, you could say something like this: "I really value your experience, your solution sounds good. Are you open to discussing ways we might add to your idea?"

The Meeting

Arrive early, have a positive attitude, and be prepared for the boss's regularly scheduled meetings.

Team meetings are a common event. They may be held multiple times a week, monthly or quarterly. The primary purpose of a team meeting is to keep everyone informed of changes, new policies and procedures, and to answer questions that may have arisen since the last meeting. Team meetings are also a time to simply bring people together face-to-face.

Whenever your team meets, condition yourself to arrive at the meeting ten to fifteen minutes early. If possible find out before the meeting what's on the agenda. During the meeting be prepared to ask a couple of pertinent questions about the topics under discussion. If possible, make a few brief comments on the subject matter. Try not to dominate the conversation—that's a very irritating behavior and may even lend some to think you are trying to run the meeting yourself. Always have paper and pen and take notes. Remember to keep a pleasant look on your face. Avoid acting or looking bored, as though you could be doing a million other things besides being in that meeting. Avoid working on things unrelated to the meeting—that's rude and unprofessional. Avoid carrying on a conversation while someone else has the floor.

If you are upset at a teammate or your boss, do not bring that attitude or negative disposition to the meeting. Act as if you're happy and at peace. Take care of whatever's bothering you outside of the meeting. If you don't like a teammate, do not show this feeling either. Avoid doing things like ignoring the person when they are speaking, or rolling your eyes, or making noises or faces that clearly show your dislike for the person.

Tennis Anyone?
Realize that being close friends with the boss can be risky.

You'll want to consider the potential implications of becoming friends with your boss outside of work. According to most experts, friendships with people at work that go beyond the office can be risky in and of themselves, especially if they are with one's boss.

These experts are not speaking here about good working relationships, but about social time spent with your manager outside of work. That, they say, should be limited. You should consider the following:

★ From your supervisor's perspective, discipline may be more difficult to administer, especially if you just hung out with him the night before.

★ Your manager's image as leader may be weakened, because people have a tendency to overlook job responsibilities when they are personal friends.

★ Your co-workers may begin to treat you differently, becoming more guarded about what they say about the boss when you are around, for example.

★ Your co-workers may question their ability to trust you— you might tell the boss what they said because the two of you are friends. You'll sense their hesitation.

He's Trippin'
Be ready for just about anything!
We'll talk more about this in a later chapter, but for now should your boss be disrespectful to you in private, let him know imme-

diately. In a very non-threatening way, let him know that you took what he said or did as an act of disrespect. Give him a chance to apologize. In your heart and mind forgive him (whether he apologizes or not, forgiveness is for you). Let him know that if something like that happens in the future, you'll contact personnel.

If an act of disrespect happens in public, find a way to respond that avoids sinking to your boss's level. You might pose as friendly a question or comment as you can muster, something like, "Excuse me, what did you mean by. . . ?" Or, "I'm sure you're not implying that. . . ." This way you let him know he's done or said something you believe is inappropriate without aggressively challenging him. The instant you are alone address the situation as above. These conversations can be difficult, especially if you don't like confrontation, but they are necessary both to the relationship and to your self-esteem.

Double Take—If you believe your boss has betrayed you in some way or you find out he's betrayed a business confidence, first make sure you have the facts—not just hearsay. Then take some time to get yourself together before you talk to him. Then, *and only then*, can you make a decision as to what to do. You can opt not to address the act of betrayal, and simply make a mental note in the future not to share certain information (if this is possible), or you can address it with him. I recommend you pose another friendly question: "I know we talked about my promotion in confidence, did you happen to mention it to Jeff?" Then let him answer. If his answer is yes, let him know (in a friendly way) that you expected him to keep that information confidential, and in the future you'd like him to honor that. This isn't a time to argue. And what you're aiming for is not necessarily that he'll tell you the truth—you pretty much already know it—you're letting him know you know he's betrayed a confidence. Regardless of the outcome, your boss will know that if you find out he's broken your confidence you're going to ask him to explain his choice. This will probably make him reconsider in the future. He may never admit his actions, or even apologize. But he'll get the point.

You need to get some points too: Where you can, avoid divulging anything you don't want others to know. Do what you want done to you: keep people's confidences. And if you suspect there's been a betrayal, but you have no solid evidence, make a mental note, keep quiet about it, and soon enough the truth will most likely surface. Then you can decide how you'll respond. Remember—some battles are won in peace and silence.

Little White Ones—If you believe your boss has lied to you or about you, again, be certain you have all the facts. Remain calm. Resist the thought of reacting verbally the moment you hear or see something contrary to what your boss has told you or led you to believe. Take some time to understand what has happened. Avoid believing one side of any story without hearing the first, second, and third side—his, yours, and the truth. When you're ready, you might approach the subject once again with a question.

For example, if your boss told you he wanted you to represent the team at the next corporate event—yet someone else's name was called—when you see him later, you might say, "You mentioned that I was your choice to represent the team at the meeting. What changed?" Receive his answer. Thank him for the explanation. Move on in peace.

If your boss has failed to give you credit for work you've done, once again, calm yourself before you make any decision about confronting the issue. At the appropriate time, a question might serve you best: "How did the group respond when you shared that the sale resulted from my presentation?" Remember: The goal is not necessarily to prove him wrong or get him to apologize or make things right. As a new hire, the goal at this point is to make him aware that you realize the rules he's playing by. Again, the goal is not his answer, admission of guilt, or apology, but simply to bring about awareness. Make a mental note. Move on in peace.

You Already Know This: Most everyone is playing to win. Your work may help someone else win. People sometimes operate under the "just apologize" principal. They know what they are doing may not be right, but they figure they can excuse their behavior by simply apologizing after the fact. A small price to pay to get what they want. Since you can't control anyone except yourself, just learn from your experiences and become an expert at managing your emotions.

Time Out !

As we close out this chapter, just a few things to consider and apply as you relate to your co-workers and those outside your immediate work group.

Mind if I Join You?
Interact outside of your comfort zone.

Once you've established friendly associations with team members and your boss, look for opportunities to extend yourself outside of the usual group of people you feel comfortable with. You might eat lunch with people from a different department— it's a little easier getting to know people over lunch. Ask questions about their career experiences. Get them to talk about themselves. Listen and learn.

Another Assist
Treat people the way you want to be treated.

Adopt this principle and your life will be much more blessed. You'll find that what you give to others and the attitude you display will be pretty much what you get back from others. For example, if and when a colleague asks for feedback on his presentation, take the opportunity to give your best advice. Offer what you know, don't hold back obvious tips that could be helpful. If you see a teammate struggling, lend him a hand. You gain the perception of being a real team player.

Also, be an encouragement. Pour courage into teammates and build them up. Be consistent about being positive. When co-workers perform well, remember to congratulate them in person. Make a point to help people feel good about the job they're doing.

Sports Talk—Every now and then throw your team-mate a no-look pass. Lob the ball above the rim so he can fly through the air for a slam dunk. Set him up to look good and you'll look good too.

Hangin' With Mr. Cooper
Associate with the well perceived.

Avoid surrounding yourself with people that are considered negative, complainers, slackers—*Run. Don't walk!*

People like this can zap your energy and even misguide you. You know what people say—birds of a feather flock together—and if you're an eagle you don't want to be flocking with crows!

Team up with those who will add value to you and the role you'll play, and those who will help you better learn your position. Make sure you have the support of your boss and respect the time you're given to learn.

Down the Hall on Your Left
Be careful what you say and <u>where</u> you say it!

Bathrooms can give you the illusion of privacy. I recommend not using the bathroom for a conference room. For starters, are you really sure you can't be heard outside the bathroom? What about the person whose desk is opposite the bathroom wall? What about the person in the fifth stall already in the bathroom? Refrain from saying anything you wouldn't want repeated. And, before you leave, wash your hands! Perception is everything, *even in the bathroom.*

The High Road
Do a quality job—always.

If you're preparing to give a presentation to one or more people, and especially if you're part of a group that's giving individual presentations, and you're told the presentation you're making is "no big deal," this is especially the time to do your best. Go the extra mile—create a slide presentation on your laptop, and be prepared to present it on a large screen. Make hard copies of the presentation in color and put the pages in a customized binder if possible. Always go the extra mile because the next guy will, and while you may know your information, you can be outdone just by the way that guy presents his information.

Before you turn in a report, check for errors. If you spot even the smallest mistake, take the time and make the correction. If the correction causes a delay, contact the recipient and be honest about the delay. Settle on a new due date if possible. There'll probably be less concern about the late report and more appreciation for a quality job.

"Let Your Yea Be Yea"
Keep your word.

You are what you say, and most of all you are what you *do*. Let your word be like gold. If you promise someone something, deliver. And deliver quickly. Avoid delaying and procrastinating. Whatever you have to do, even if you realize you've over committed and don't feel you can deliver, try above all else to deliver what you committed to. Think about what you are saying you will do and where you will be, and then take the steps to do it and be there.

If you tell a client that you'll call at 10:00, call at 10:00. If you tell a teammate you'll help him from 5:30 to 6:00, be on time and keep your word. If you tell a customer you'll call back to follow up, be specific about the day and time and call back. If you tell a customer you'll mail something out to them, do it quickly. If you tell your boss you'll have the information he needs by 1:00, have it by then or earlier. One of the most powerful perceptions you can build for yourself is that you are a person of your word.

It Was All His Fault
Let others admit their own mistakes.

Publicly spotlighting a co-worker's blunder is not a good idea.

You run the risk of being perceived as insecure—not what you want. If you have to comment, recognize the need to move forward and focus on a solution. Assuming others are aware of the mistake, instead of focusing on or even mentioning it, you might ask, "Where do we go from here?" Even though you may be competing for some of the same things, in the end you are still teammates and there should be some loyalty there.

You Can Never Be Sure
Treat co-workers as if one day you could work for them.

When you're asked for information, offer it willingly and promptly. Thank the requester for seeking your input, and invite him to let you know how else you might help. Like an unexpected relative, the day will come when you'll be interviewing for a position on the previous "requester's" team. Let's go back to the information you were asked for earlier—you know, the email you blew off sending until you had time but never got back to. When you're asking the requester for a position on the team, think about how you're going to answer the requester's questions about teamwork and support.

Market to the Manager
Look for ways to market yourself for future positions.

At some point you may be interested in moving to another area of the company. This is the time to begin habits that will help prepare your way. Start small and plan to be noticed (unassumingly). When you have the opportunity, be genuine in finding out the business goals and business issues of the hiring manager in the department where you want to work. As you begin to be perceived as successful, you might offer one or two ideas to help solve the hiring manager's business challenges. Hallway and elevator conversations should go from general, idle talk about sports or politics or your weekend, to offering a business solution or simple idea. Recommend business solutions when you're out to lunch or taking a break at a company meeting.

Make this a habit. You'll be perceived and remembered as adding value.

Larry, an account executive, has an interest in someday joining the marketing department. Joe is a successful marketing manager. Success stories of Joe and his marketing team frequently make headlines in the company newsletter. With each story, Larry forwards a note of personal congratulations. Larry thanks Joe and his team for the support they give him in his sales efforts. For the upcoming newsletter, Larry plans to share a success story based on the support Joe's team provided.—You get the point, right?

All right, hit the locker room. It's halftime . . .

My Personal Notes

Take a few minutes and make note of any information that stood out:

_____

_____

_____

_____

_____

_____

_____

What will you do differently as a result of what you've read?

_____

_____

_____

_____

_____

_____

_____

Halftime | Before You Return, Tighten Up Your Game

The first half of the game buzzed with activities and hard play. You're working the floor. You're playing your position well, and you're playing by the rules. Now it's halftime. At this point, you've got a little time to rest. While you're gathering yourself, we'll talk about the next area of focus: your overall performance.

How well you do your job and the attitudes you display are more significant than your "potential" to do well or your skills and talents. This is the time when all your opponents are cleared out of your way and you have a chance to make your individual move to the basket to put points on the board in the area of individual performance. You've got a chance to blow out your stats in the area of perception building.

Consider the following, and when you return to the game for the third and fourth quarters, you'll finish strong and win.

Isolation Offense
Understand performance appraisals.

Measuring work performance is a concept that's been around for over eighty years—sounds like it's here to stay in some form or another. Every year, what you do and how you do it are reviewed, with mid-year and year-end evaluations usually tracking and recording your progress. Individual performance is reviewed and rated. Ratings are grounds for many things—good and not so good. Generally, you get more money for doing an outstanding job; you get to keep your job for doing what's expected; you get a chance to improve so you *can* have a job; and you can lose your job for not completing the minimum requirements.

Most evaluations are formally recorded, reviewed by you and your boss, signed by you and your boss, and forwarded to Human Resources to become a permanent statement of your work. This permanent reflection of your accomplishments is what speaks for you before you arrive or say a word. If you interview for other positions within your company, the hiring manager may request copies of your last few appraisals as part of the interview or to make decisions about you that can affect your interview, positively or negatively.

The Name Game
Find out the name of the performance appraisal.

Depending upon where you work and what you do, the names of the event/process/measurement tool could vary: Performance Review, Performance Appraisal, Performance Evaluation, Performance Agreement, Pay-for-Performance Plan, Performance Management, 360-degree Feedback, Continuous Improvement Reviews (CIR). The rating system for each may vary as well.

For more details on the last three processes, refer to Appendix 6.

Parts and Pieces

Know the elements of the performance appraisal.

In general, you're given an overall rating of how well you perform your job. The overall rating or evaluation is calculated by how well you scored in every element deemed necessary to complete your job description. You've been given the opportunity to do your job—exceeding, meeting, or failing to meet what's expected. The measured elements can be defined by the company or by a combination of company and employee. Categories usually include what you did (competencies and skills) and the way you performed your job (behaviors and attitudes).

The Title Belongs to You

Prior to appraisal time, review the appraisal with your boss.

Two keys to a successful performance review: Knowing the process and owning the process. Get a copy of the actual performance appraisal that outlines what you're being measured against for the year. Schedule to meet with your boss well in advance of the actual review to examine the actual process—to understand how and for what you'll be judged. Review your objectives, share your understanding of the measurements, and ask your boss to give you clear examples as well. You want to walk away knowing what you'll be measured against and making sure you and the boss share the same understanding.

Post Up and Make Your Moves Count—Now that you understand the measurements, you'll want to put together an Action Plan *(feel free to use the sample at the end of Appendix 5)* to overachieve in every category of performance. Present the Action Plan to your boss. Prepare an outline of the areas where you'll want his involvement to help attain your goals. Again, check for understanding and clarification and gain the boss's commitment. Your goals should be aligned with your boss's overall goals, with his boss's goals, and with the company's goals.

Your Best, Nothing Less

Have some passion about your work!

Do your best. Bring a level of intensity to all you do. I'm not saying be fake, I'm saying carry out your assignment in a way that makes a difference. When things are tough—and they sometimes will be—instead of acting defeated, though the challenge appears overwhelming, become passionate about finding a solution. And you will. Execute your plan with courage and confidence, asking for assistance where needed but taking ownership for what you have been tasked to do.

How Many Boards Did You Pull Down?

Keep files of your own performance.

Keep a file of all completed activities. Don't make the mistake of expecting that your boss will remember everything you've done—or that you'll remember it all yourself at the end of the year. Ultimately, it's up to you to know what you've done. You'll need this during review time.

Watch the Shot Clock—Be aware of where you are in the year and what you're supposed to have accomplished by a certain time during the year. Apart from your mid-year review, agree to meet with your boss quarterly (at a minimum) to assess your progress.

Use the Performance Appraisal Tracking document in Appendix 7 to check your progress.

Your Turn

Rate yourself.

When it's time to review the year's performance, give yourself at least a week to put together in written form your own review rating, attaching any supporting documents. For each category, calculate how well you performed based on the facts, and rate yourself. As an example, if you were required to complete five activities, total the number you completed based on evidence and then rate how well you did. If you completed 10 rather than five, you overachieved and scored 200 percent of what you were asked to do. At review time, you'll want to bring the rating and evidence with you. Remember: The review is generally a two-way affair—it includes not only your manager's feedback but yours as well.

Fireworks Are For the 4th

No matter how the actual review is going—well or not so well—keep your professional composure.

This can be a very volatile time. After all, someone is actually telling you their observation of how well or how poorly they think you're doing. Observations, opinions, beliefs, and perceptions can vary at any time. Try to remember that this is a review of your work, not necessarily a review of *you*. Not taking comments and feedback personally is tough, but this is not the time to allow your ego or self-esteem to be altered. This is why evidence of your work is so key. In a professional way, you can prove your observation and beliefs about your own performance. During the formal review, allow your manager to present his feedback.

Show Time!

When your boss finishes, ask for permission to review what you've prepared.

Go back over each category. Hopefully, his assessment will be in line with yours. If there are areas you believe weren't considered, present the information. If your activities warrant a higher rating, ask for the change. Preparing your own rating and comparing the two reviews makes for a very professional exchange and assessment. Having the facts eliminates the potential for the scene to turn emotional. I'm not suggesting you'll agree on everything. Because you're two different people, there's an excellent chance you'll see things differently no matter what. I'm saying that documentation helps the two of you at least *agree* you're seeing some of the same things differently.

John Hancock
You can sign or not sign.

Now comes time to sign the appraisal. If you agree with the review rating this is easy. Sign, keep a copy, and file it. But let's say you and your boss can't reach an agreeable rating and you believe you have the documented evidence warranting additional consideration. You have a couple of choices: If the overall appraisal rating is acceptable to you, but an element in a certain category is not—and you want to submit the truer reflection of your work—submit your documentation, sign the review, and check the box that says "employee comments attached." If there's no such box, write directly on the form, "employee comments attached," and initial. At a minimum, your documentation goes in your file and your attachments will serve as additional information.

Not Quite
If your overall appraisal rating is not acceptable to you, you could ask your boss to reconsider his ratings per your attachments.

If he is unwilling to change the overall rating, let him know you're not ready to sign the review. Let him know that while you respect his opinions, you believe your work deserves a second look. Let him know in a nice way that you'd like to take the next step in presenting your case in order to request an overall rating change. You may not actually have to go this far, but be prepared if this is really important to you. State in writing that based on the review results, you'd like to change your rating. If your boss is unwilling to offer you a way to have your rating reconsidered, let him know you'll be contacting his boss or personnel for guidance. Being as friendly as you can, go through the process and push for what you believe to be right. After all, this is a permanent reflection of your work. As long as you have the facts, push for the change.

It's Not the End of the World

Review time is not a time to act like you hate your boss.

Remember: He is still your boss. Remember: He can still make life at work a little tougher if he wants to. So keep a great attitude about things. Be open to hearing him.

Every performance review isn't a bad experience. If you do have difficulties with the review experience, try to remain positive about what you know to be your contributions. If you've really done the best job you're capable of, don't allow anyone or any measurement process to defeat you. No one is perfect, and that's not the goal. Just do your best and find a way to show this the way management needs to see it. If your first year's rating was not what you wanted, make a difference next year.

You're not always going to be judged solely on the work you do. Perception is as much a part of your performance as your skills and attitudes. If you're perceived as valuable, you are valuable. Combine that perception with your skills and attitudes, and you'll be a solid player. Can you see now why doing so many things to maintain the image you want is so vital to your overall success?

Now that you've gotten your second wind, you're ready to get back in the game. You're focused. You're charged. Go!

My Personal Notes

Take a few minutes and make note of any information that stood out:

_____
_____
_____
_____
_____
_____
_____
_____

What will you do differently as a result of what you've read?

_____
_____
_____
_____
_____
_____
_____
_____

3Q | Before You "Go-Go," Consider Where You're *Trying* to Go

Every aspect of your performance counts. This includes what you reveal at the office about your personal life outside of work, and how you socialize at work. Though you may figure these two things don't matter much, the fact is they do.

Think about a certain basketball player. Definitely talented and certainly highly skilled. His rebounding and defense on the court were exceptional. This same high performer dyed his hair colors that weren't even on the chart. He wore women's clothes. He displayed a zillion tattoos and a ring hanging from his nose. No one doubted his ability to play basketball, but you didn't hear his teammates bragging about being his running buddy, nor did you hear the coaching staff label him the team role model.

The point: Though you may be eccentric, open-minded, creative and all that, work really isn't the place to offer the details of your personal life and flaunt your social "soul-ness bold-ness."

Use this quarter to build a respectable perception.

Less is *More* Better

Be general about your personal life.

"Guy talk" is something that needs to be closely monitored in the work setting. Talking "shop," getting loud about your favorite sports team, bragging on your own golf game—these are all part of the normal fun of work life and are not a real problem. But when it comes to your most personal, private life, be careful. It's fine that people know you're married, engaged, or dating. But they don't need to know your marriage is suffering, your engagement has been called off several times, or that you're seeing several women at the same time.

You need to take a very mature approach to the way you present your personal life. Though a man's reputation can sometimes survive long after rumors or bad press, it's not wise to feed fire with fuel. The fact that you have a personal life is important, the details are not. Discussing the play you and your wife saw is great. Telling co-workers about the fight you had during intermission is not. You could share the news that your wife's expecting, but you don't have to tell everyone that she's going to have a natural childbirth and breastfeed. That type of information is just not necessary for people to know.

If you're being pressed to reveal gooey details of your life, you can simply say you'd rather not say or kindly blow them off by saying, "Oh, you know me, always having a good time." Sometimes, simply not offering information during these kinds of discussions is enough to let people know you're a private person.

E-News!

Realize that some people may have hidden motives for wanting to know the details of your personal life.

There are always "the curious ones." You know, people (male and female) whose sole purpose in life is to get the goods on their co-workers. Some people do this because they are looking to gain an edge in the workplace and will use any means to do so.

Be aware, no matter how nice you are, or how nice people seem to be, there may be some who do not have your best interests at heart. When you're being asked a lot of personal questions, think about who's asking. Is this a person who gossips with you about other people? If so, understand that *whatever* you tell them will likely be repeated. Consider this: Anything you tell anyone has the potential to be told to someone else. For instance, you might get asked (in private, in front of a group, or even by your manager) what you did over the weekend or even the night before. There's simply no need to say things like, "Oh God, I'm so tired. We went out last night and whew!" Or, "I'm so exhausted! I have the biggest hangover. Last night was incredible. We went to this club, we got our drink on. . . ." Or, "I am so waxed from last night. I don't know if I can make it. I can't wait to go home so I can sleep off my hangover." Or, "I worked at my second job until three this morning. Man, I'm just hanging on."

Little Tongue, Big Trouble
Refrain from using profanity.

No matter how comfortable you feel at work, whether there's an office full of people or whether you're working late and there are only one or two people with you, avoid cursing. The moment you utter a curse word, people's perception about you dances all over the perception chart. A curse word can linger in a person's mind and conjure up ideas about you long after you've left the room. Using profanity is inappropriate in the workplace anyway. Just avoid it altogether.

O.K., That's Enough
Refrain from flirting with co-workers.

Flirting should be put to rest. From a male (or female) perspective, flirting does nothing for your professional image.

"I Think I Love You"

If you have a crush on someone in your office, for the time being, keep your feelings to yourself.

Here's another area to practice maturity and wisdom. You may be unable to avoid being attracted to someone, but let's just say there isn't the same tolerance in the workplace for such interest as there may have been in the past. As harmless as you may think you're being you should keep your personal feelings to yourself at this time. If you have a crush on a young lady at work, consider simply getting to know her from afar before diving in to tell her your initial feelings. You might go out to lunch with a group of people—including her, or you might sit at the same table during company events.

The point is, instead of falling all over her at work—which is inappropriate and can be misunderstood as harassment—calm down and breathe a little. A crush is something you "think" you have—you usually feel that way right after you've just met or have been in her presence briefly. However, you may *think* you like her only because you have little to no evidence on which to *think* otherwise. Nothing wrong with thoughts. But you might want to keep your thoughts to yourself and take your time to get to know her along with your other co-workers. Be mature. You can wait until you've spent enough time to know some basics about who she is, if she's available, if she's interested, and if you still like what you've discovered instead of what you thought. Remember keeping your feelings to yourself also means *not* telling your boys at work what you'd like to do with this woman, so on and so forth. Again, exercise maturity. If you've crossed the line of infatuation and confessed all your initial feelings to your boys or to the young lady, there's still time to recover. Slowly begin to back off. Maintain more of a business tone when you talk, be polite but try not to be too giddy. You can slowly back your way out of too much intensity and enter into a calm acquaintance. Really use this time as a new hire to establish yourself and build the foundation of a clean, solid, professional perception. Often, office crushes can get you off focus and distracted from your goals.

Bon Voyage
Attend going-away parties.

If invited, attend going-away parties, even if you don't know the person. Making the person who's leaving feel their efforts were appreciated is important. And if you didn't have the best working relationship, a going-away party could be a fence mender—time to make a fresh start.

Get Your Groove On *Right*
Remember people are watching you at office parties and social events.

Attendance is important at office parties and company events. You want to be perceived as sociable. At company social events, unless told otherwise, plan to stay for at least 45 minutes and no longer than an hour after the mandatory time requirement. Have a purpose in mind—use the time to get to know people, to build relationships and alliances. Listen and learn. Decide your networking strategy. Target at least three people you're going to introduce yourself to and find out about their background, work experience, goals, and aspirations. Use the time for more than just a good meal, drinks, and a good time. Be purposeful.

Just for Drills—No matter how gorgeous you think a woman is or how much you like her, do not hit on her at a social business event. Even if you perceive her to be hitting on you, be polite, accept her compliments, but keep a level business mind.

Mr. Manners
Eat and drink with manners.

If food is formally served, eat what you're given and don't ask the table staff for a second helping. If the meal is buffet-style, put small amounts of food on your plate. Try not to have food piled up or falling off the edge. This should not be your first and only meal of the day.

If alcohol is offered, I recommend that you not drink—but if you must, limit the drink to one glass, preferably wine. Remember to eat before your one drink, not after. Steer clear of mixed drinks—they can take your personality to another level.

John Travolta
Have a good time, but keep it conservative.

Company socials are a time to have fun—good food, laughs, and a little dancing are good for the soul. Now a word about dancing: *In this context*, dancing should be a time to have a *little* fun. It's not the same as dancing at the club or even at home when your favorite songs are playing. At company events, although the music may be tempting you to let yourself go, remember you're being watched, and perceptions are being formed, opinions made.

How do you know if your dancing is inappropriate for a company event? Unless you're doing the waltz, and even if it's with your spouse, *in this setting*, it's inappropriate if your hands are on someone; if your hands are on yourself; if a body part of yours is touching a body part of the person you're dancing with; if your dancing partner is touching a body part of yours; if you're sweating like you're at a frat party; if you're out of breath; if people are looking at you from every direction; if your moves are creating a draft; if you have done the equivalent of a squat; if you're sliding and bending and dipping at more than a 45 degree angle—any of these is a clue that your dancing is inappropriate. Also avoid slow dancing with co-workers altogether. Remember dancing at company events is not the same as what you may be used to, so you may have to make an adjustment and save your gift to cut a step for another time.

The Cat's Away, the Mouse Will Play—Overnight conferences, out-of-town meetings, conventions, and reward trips can be a danger zone for the new hire. Be careful and on extra guard. Remember, no matter how beautiful the resort and no matter how great the accommodations, technically you're still at work. Though reward trips are a celebration of your personal hard work, you have not earned the right to let it *all hang out.*

Socialize, network, and return to your room before the next morning (midnight). Whatever is going on after midnight, your presence is not a business requirement. If you're invited to go off the premises, just say, "Thank you for the offer, but no thank you." The pressure to fit in is great, but resist. Go to your room and go to bed—alone. Keep your hotel room number to yourself. This is not conquest time. You are a professional and you're in charge of keeping it that way. If it's the last night of the trip or if it's the closing affair, staying a little beyond midnight is acceptable.

Another Word to the Wise—When alcohol is present at these events, and husbands are not, a female co-worker who is attracted to you may share her personal interests in "getting to know you." If someone is making advances to get to know you better, go ahead and draw the line. As you are revealing your line, be considerate, firm, but unapologetic.

Poolside Manners—Be conscious of your body and avoid any indecent exposure. Avoid wearing or doing anything that would not enhance your professional image.

Sex, Drugs and Rock 'n Roll—Avoid intimate relationships with co-workers, especially with your boss, unless, of course, the two of you are married. Affairs with married people at work are, naturally, unprofessional. Say no to drugs. Rock—but watch where you roll.

My Personal Notes

Take a few minutes and make note of any information that stood out:

_____

_____

_____

_____

_____

_____

_____

_____

What will you do differently as a result of what you've read?

_____

_____

_____

_____

_____

_____

_____

4Q | Before You Celebrate, Play 'til The Buzzer Sounds

In addition to trying to get your work done, there's "workplace gaming" going on—co-workers making all kinds of moves to get in a better position to win. So this final quarter is the time to give it all you have.

Down to the last second, play to win. Play the type of defense that protects your ideas and increases your overall value as an employee and a team player. Rebound in the areas of personal weaknesses, ranging from improving technical skills to managing anger or frustration. Release early so you can be open for a slam-dunk by relating well to your co-workers when asking for assistance or requesting information. Take a charge by choosing useful methods of communication. Go around set picks, or run outside the traps when you see one coming so you can make moves to blow past your co-workers with character and poise.

The most was saved for last.

It's All About *Me*
Realize, just as you do, co-workers have an agenda.

Keep in mind that everyone has an agenda—their reason for doing what they are doing. Realize everyone competes to accomplish their own agenda. Because you're not always sure what someone else is trying to accomplish, and because you cannot under any circumstance control other people's behavior, you've got to focus on how you can maintain your professional image while accomplishing your own agenda. Learning to control yourself and recognizing other people's agendas are two things that will help you make favorable decisions and choices for yourself.

Workplace Gaming 101
Recognize the game you're in.

As you know, competition is going on all day, every day, in the workplace. What do I mean by competition? You know—workplace gaming—the contest where everybody's trying to be the winner. For now, let's just say it's between new hires (though gaming can include co-workers who are not new hires). Basically, you're in a game where everyone's trying to stand out, impress, be in the lead. What does this competition look like? Everyone has their own style—some are bold and outspoken, some are quiet (but deadly), some ask a lot of questions about how you're doing things but rarely share their own tactics, some are silly acting but secretly serious, others are confident, appearing to be natural leaders.

They are your teammates who have to get the first word in on everything (all the time), who are experts at everything, who make recommendations to solve problems no one has thought of yet, who sit by the boss every chance they get, who are obsessed with out-performing everyone (even if it's by a sliver), who create the best presentations, who try to be picked for all the special assignments, who make the most comments at the team meetings, who stay late or come in early and chat it up with the boss, and on and on and *on*. This is the competition I'm talking about. As you know, the contest is *on*. See the game for what it is—play, play smart, and don't whine.

Heads or Tails?

View others in the workplace as "friendly competitors."

You are playing (at those things we mentioned earlier) to win and you have opponents (earlier referred to as competitors). One way to keep a smile on your face while dealing with the competition is to view co-workers as "friendly competitors."

Remember the contest we talked about? The one where your co-workers (male or female) are trying to keep up with what you're doing, presenting their ideas during the team meetings and to the boss all the time, positioning themselves to be the team leader, spending a good deal of time talking to the boss, taking advantage of every opportunity to be seen with the boss. *These* co-workers are your friendly competitors and, just like you, they are out to win.

When your friendly competitor makes a move against you, don't be too alarmed. Realize that using you in some way may be what it takes for that person to win.

Need an Example? Okay. Suppose your friendly competitor wants to receive the next promotion. He (male or female) knows you're perceived to be professional and mentally prepared for the same promotion. He may believe that potentially you're interested in the job as well. Your friendly competitor might feel he stands a better chance at getting that promotion if he can get your boss to question your level of commitment to the job.

His Possible Game Plan & Tactics: So let's say he knows you perform at jazz clubs on the weekends. Don't be surprised if your friendly competitor starts asking you questions about your gigs, and mentioning your commitment to music in front of your boss (either in your presence or not). Know that his job is to try to use any advantage he thinks he can use. He's guarding you.

He's waving his hands in your face to try and block your vision and your ability to make a good shot.

What to Do? Your job is to be aware of the tactics and go around him. You do this, first, by recognizing the game. I'm not saying that behind every question there is an agenda. What I am saying is that you need to act like that's the case, and be sure not to give out any information you think could be used against you now or later. You've got to be expecting his defense and planning your next move ahead of his. Think about how you're going to respond. Are you going to engage your friendly competitor in conversation? Are you going to get angry at his tactic and lose your cool? No. Getting angry at your friendly competitor for using his tactics would suggest that you're unprepared for the real game you're in. Your image may suffer. Just as in a real game, when you get angry with someone for making a good move, the other players start laughing. They view that type of anger as childish. Remember hearing players say, "It's just a game?" Well, they're right. *It's just a game.*

Your Move? You're playing to win. You're going to give him a head fake and go the other way. Remember what your friendly competitor knows about you, anticipate his tactics, and prepare responses before he arrives at your cubicle or asks question in a team meeting. You're probably going to say something like this, "Oh, you know I've been focusing so much on my commitments at work that I spend much of my weekend preparing for the up-coming week."

Well Watson . . .

Protect your ideas.

Present your own ideas. If you're onto something really good, let your boss know, ask him to keep it confidential, and instead of broadcasting your thoughts around the office, simply develop the plan and present it. I've watched co-workers take other people's ideas and run with them and score all over the place. Remember the words *agenda* and *friendly competitors*.

Fake It Until You Make It
Improve areas where you struggle.

If you're aware that making group presentations isn't one of your strong points, don't avoid the issue (like calling in sick the day you have to present, or by continuing to do a poor job just because right now you're no good at it). Find ways to improve the skill. Practice in front of the mirror, take a class outside of work—whatever you do, get the help you need and work on the skill until you're stronger.

Hmm . . .
It's O.K. to ask for assistance.

There's nothing wrong with asking for clarification or under-standing. As men, realize it's O.K. to *not* know everything *and* it's O.K. to ask for help. There are great ways to get the help you need. The key is to *ask*. If you resort to making a joke out of your own request for help, that's O.K. too. Regardless of your approach, ask. It's O.K.

I Understand vs. I *Don't* Understand
Keep your power by using empowering words.

Empowering words will help you sound intelligent and ex-pert. Practice using expressions such as "I understand" (instead of I don't understand), "I believe" (instead of I don't think), "I'm aware of"(instead of I never knew about that), "I know" (instead of I don't know), "I'll give it some thought" (instead of I have no idea).

When you're unsure about something ask empowering ques-tions like, "*I understand* how you came up with such and such, what did you include in part five of your analysis?" You'll want to avoid saying things like, "I'm really confused. I don't know what to do at all. What do you think I should do?" Saying something like this causes one to wonder if you're going to need help with everything.

I'll Take Care of That
Volunteer.

Here's a place to be aggressive (this is an area your friendly competitor will try and dominate as well). Volunteer to handle certain tasks that may result from unexpected business needs. Let's say an idea is presented in a team meeting and the boss needs someone to be the contact person or to take the lead in managing the activity. Raise your hand. You now have an additional chance to demonstrate your skills and talents. You're also able to strengthen the perception that you are trustworthy and responsible, someone to be counted on. Confirm acceptance of the task by email, and update your boss by email as well (outline the activity and the success of the assignment). This way you have documentation to show your volunteering spirit and initiative. Keep copies of these updates and use them during performance appraisal time when you need to show your stuff. If the activity gets put on hold for some reason, the email copies can still be used to demonstrate your volunteer spirit.

Also, find something that needs to be done before others do, even before your boss does. Volunteering for something that no one has done before demonstrates initiative and makes you more visible. Also, periodically volunteer to cover for a teammate or your boss while they're out on vacation. Learning more than your job is valuable as well.

Do You Mind?
Accept special assignments.

Additionally, if your boss asks *you* to handle a special project or take a special assignment outside of your normal job responsibilities, gladly accept. Even if you don't want to do it, don't have the time to do it, *agree* to do it. Gain agreement on the objectives, resources and due date.

If you find the workload impossible, you might consider getting permission to be relieved of a few duties to take on the special assignment. Accepting assignments outside your typical job is beneficial in several ways: Your management and leadership skills are being evaluated, you're gaining success and recognition, and you're becoming valuable. Value adds power. So when you're asked to handle special assignments, "yes" is your answer.

Ask Him, He Knows All About That . . .
Become a specialist or an expert in some aspect of your job.

Mitchell decided to become an expert in using Powerpoint software to create dynamic and powerful presentations. He became efficient at importing files and graphics to make detailed and complex information easier to understand. Mitchell became so well known for his Powerpoint presentations, he became the team's main resource. His ability had been noticed by a region marketing manager who asked him to help with a company presentation. Everybody knew that if Mitchell wanted a job in the marketing department, his reputation for pulling together outstanding Powerpoint presentations gave him a great shot at getting at least an interview.

It's Shine Time!
Make yourself visible (just not overbearing).

Stay in tune with the fact that for the most part you'll need to manage your own visibility within the company. Your friendly competitors are doing the same thing. Don't expect that people will just know you are brilliant and have off-the-chart ideas. If you've come up with a unique solution, send an email to your boss letting him know what you put together, and invite him to pass it along to the team. If possible, ask if you can present the information at a team meeting to answer any questions.

At the same time, be creative in the way you self-advertise.

You don't want to look like the teacher's pet, running to your boss every time you do something well. But you can put copies of your work on your teammates' desk (and a copy for your boss letting him know what you passed out) with a note that says you thought the information might be helpful. Or you can put together a presentation and make it available to the team (make sure your boss is clued in). Of course, doing these things tends to bring on even more competition from others. They'll figure out what you're doing and try doing the same thing. But it's O.K., you'll just have to try and beat them to it every time. The worst that could happen is that a lot of great ideas start surfacing—and everything is right about that!

Things That Go Boom!
Avoid showing anger or extreme frustration.

In every situation, no matter how valid your anger is, do whatever you must to remain calm and collected. When you explode in anger, or otherwise react in a highly charged manner, several perceptions are created: you're too aggressive, you need to be stopped, you're immature—you're just not qualified to handle the job.

Excuse yourself when you realize you're headed for extreme anger. You'll know when you're losing it—your voice starts rising, sweat starts breaking out under your arms. If you're seated, you'll find yourself sitting up. If you're standing, you'll move forward or backward.

Personal Foul—If you do lose your temper (it usually happens at least once), give yourself time to recover. There's no need to walk around acting like your were right. Even if your point was correct, your behavior was not. You don't need to act like a puppy trying to make up after messing on the carpet, but a little humility, even if it's only expressed by your tone of voice, might be helpful. There's also no need to focus on the event. Pick a time when you're settled down before you try to finish the initial meeting or conversation that set you off. If it's helpful to avoid the face-to-face aspect of the conversation, instead call or send an email.

The Co-Worker Family
Be conscious of how you're relating to others when you're asking for assistance or requesting information.

In addition to your boss, you'll have what I call a "co-worker group." As a new hire, these are people you'll probably have the most contact with. The co-worker group consists of teammates, counterparts (peers who may not be on your team but work for the company and do the same job you do), resource or support people (those whose work ultimately provides a service to many, including you), other managers or directors, and executives (including their assistants). At the executive level, anything other than an acquaintance will be unlikely during your new-hire stage. Out of the co-worker group, most of your day-to-day contact will be with teammates, and with resource or support people.

Regardless if it's your boss or someone in your co-worker group, and regardless of their titles, there's a certain level of common respect you want to offer when you're asking for assistance or requesting information to help you complete your job.

Be Grateful
Don't assume people "should" do things for you.

Now let's look at your attitude. For starters, when you're asking for help or requesting information, your attitude has to be correct. When I hear people say, "Well he gets paid to do such and such . . ." they sound as though their attitude is that someone owes them something. As though that very fact alone should be enough to make the other person do what they want done. It's not that people aren't getting paid to provide a service, it's really about the disrespectful style you'll have if you approach a person feeling they *should* do something for you. If you take the attitude that you'd be most grateful *if* they did something, your

approach is probably going to be more respectful. And others
will probably feel better about doing what you ask—even if they
are supposed to.

I Need You to Do This. Now!

Avoid walking up to people and just jumping right into asking for
assistance or requesting information.

The next thing to consider is your approach. Respect others'
time and the tasks they need to complete. Their priorities may
not be yours (usually they are not) and their performance review
may not specifically include giving you the help you need. With
this understanding, first ask if they have a moment *(and remem-*
ber you don't have to apologize for approaching them). Tell them
you need their assistance, ask if you could interrupt *(and you*
don't have to say you hate to bother them, or interrupt them—that
isn't necessary either). Respect their answer. Usually you'll be
given the go-ahead to ask, and then they'll let you know if your
request is something they can do right then. At least you've begun to discuss what you'll need.

If you go to someone's work area and they're on the phone,
make eye contact to let them know you would like their attention. If after a minute or so they don't acknowledge your presence,
or motion for you to wait, don't continue to stand there. Go back
later.

The point here is that there's a certain way to approach
people, and especially in the workplace, where so much depends
on teamwork. The way you treat people usually becomes the way
they treat you. When asking for assistance or requesting information, be respectful, be considerate, and be willing to ask more
than just one person for what you need.

Uh . . .

Know __what__ you're asking, and what you're asking __for__.

First you need to be clear on what asking for help could
possibly mean. So when you're asking, you're aware of what type

of help you're really asking for. There are categories of what's considered help. There's easy stuff (names, numbers) which usually takes a few minutes of someone's time. Then there's the more involved stuff, when someone has to invest personal energy and more than a few minutes to help you.

Be clear about what you need. Do you need to know who handles a particular job responsibility (their name and number)? Do you need a second opinion regarding a presentation you're putting together? Do you need help solving a business issue or advice as to how to get started on a new task? Do you need help learning how to sort data in an Excel spreadsheet or do you need to know how to create the entire spreadsheet? Do you need help getting in touch with someone who hasn't responded? Be clear about what you're asking and what you're asking for.

High and Low
Know __when__ to ask for help.

As a general rule, before you ask for help, try your best to find what you need yourself. Exhaust the resources made available to you. If nothing else, this will help you be more specific about what type of help you need. O.K., *now* you can justify asking people in your co-worker group (beginning with your teammates, counterparts, resource or support people). If you still need assistance, as a last resort, ask your boss.

Also realize there's a difference between asking for assistance or information from your boss, on the one hand, and from teammates, counterparts, resource or support people, and managers, directors or executives.

In General
Know __when__ to request information.

Before requesting information from your co-worker group or your boss, think about whether the information you need is readily available. And just as in asking for assistance—look for it yourself. When all else fails, ask someone to "point you in the right direction." Another important consideration is the provider's time. If there's any part of the information you can get on your own, do so. You'll want to ask immediately, not waiting until your last minute and then rushing them. Don't confuse *your* waiting until the last minute with someone else's failure to respond fast enough. Of course, if you're making an urgent request for time-sensitive information that was asked of you because of an unexpected crisis—that's another matter. Some situations create a rush, and if this is the case, advise the person of the unexpected nature of the request.

About an Hour

Be sensitive to the time your request might require.

You'll want to ask the information provider if he has a few minutes, either right then or later in the day or week. Be honest about how much time you'll need and stick to that time unless you've asked permission to extend it. Otherwise, they might put you off the next time because they'll feel they were tricked into having a longer meeting with you than you originally asked for. Try to remove the feeling of creating more work for the other person. Keep in mind how you feel when you're asked to interrupt your regular work to provide someone else with information.

Bull's Eye

Know __what__ information you're requesting.

Be sure you are clear about a few things. Work-related information falls into a couple of categories as well. Information can be in the form of a tangible document (something you need to have a copy of or something that needs to be created). Information could also be something like process flows or facts, figures, and updates (things that reside in someone else's mind). Information, as with asking for assistance, can be something relatively easy (a copy of something already done) or more time-consuming (creating something).

And so for your own sense of clarity and efficiency you need to know a few things. *What kind of information are you looking for?* Is a verbal answer all you need? Or do you really want copies of existing documentation, like a completed spreadsheet or form? *Why you need it?* Do you need it for your files, to give to someone else, or to meet a real business requirement? *Who do you need it from?* Do you need the information from someone in your co-worker group, or from your boss? *What will you or the person you're requesting information from need to do?* Will you need to forward a form to the information provider to complete and return to you? Or will you need the provider to pull together information that doesn't already exist? *And how do you want the information delivered?* Can this information be sent electronically?

All these considerations are important because they'll help you be clear about exactly what you're requesting. And being this thorough also helps those people you work with who seem to always have "a need to know" because knowing helps them think through their own work more clearly. A note here: When you ask your boss for information, definitely explain why you need what you need from him, not so much to justify the request, but because he may know a more efficient and productive way.

Standard Operating Procedures
Find out the process for making requests.

For standard information requests—and you'll need to find out what's considered standard—find out the process, beginning with who do you ask? Understand the turn-around time: How long will the answer take? And plan accordingly: Allow enough time for the person you're asking to get back to you as well as the time it will take you to meet your own deadline.

For ideas and specific advice about ways to ask for help and request information from your co-worker group and your boss, review Appendix 8.

Did You Have a Chance to . . .
Follow up with respect.

If you've asked for help, or requested information from someone in your co-worker group or from your boss and they haven't gotten back to you, be patient and understanding. You may have to get what you need elsewhere. Avoid showing frustration or impatience when you're not given what you've asked for. Learn from the experience. Adjust your game. Be cool and think. Work through these situations, stick to the facts, and stay away from how you feel about what's going on. When a person is not responding to your request, it's better if you assume that it's due to a mistake, a misunderstanding, or an unintentional oversight, but not because they don't want to or don't like you. Don't retaliate, especially when people in your co-worker group or your boss fail to do what they committed to do, or don't respond to your follow-up. Think about the response you want from the person involved. If you decide to mention the situation, have the type of conversation that will solicit the outcome you desire.

When it's your boss who hasn't gotten back to you, assume he hasn't received your messages, or hasn't had an opportunity to get to you yet. Minus the chill when you finally speak to him— be prepared to start your request from the very beginning, as if it's the first time you're bringing it up.

Refer back to Appendix 8 for reminders of ways to ask for assistance or request information from your boss. For follow-up ideas and details, refer to Appendix 9.

I'd Like to Speak to Your Boss Please
Know when to take an unresolved issue to someone else's boss— and let the person know your plans to do so.

Speaking to someone's boss can be referred to as "going over someone's head." Before doing this, do everything else you can to resolve the issue yourself. Approach the person yourself, or ask your boss for advice or assistance in resolving the matter. If you still get nowhere, try my "three times you're out" rule—at the third request, they're out, their boss is in. When you've exhausted your other options, ask the person who their boss is, and let them know you'll be speaking with that person. You might even invite them to be present. After all, you're not trying to get anyone in trouble, you're trying to get what you need done, *done*.

It's Elevator Time—An example of when you might ask to speak to someone's boss—Let's say your paycheck is incorrect. You've spoken to your boss about the concern and he's given you the go-ahead to resolve it with personnel. You talk to a personnel assistant who says he's fixed the problem, and you'll have what you're owed in a week. A week goes by, no check. You repeat the process. A second week goes by, no check. At this point, it's time to get in touch with the director of personnel. Speak to the assistant the third time to let him know you appreciate his help so far, but that your issue is not resolved—you have no corrected check. Let him know you will be speaking to the director and welcome him to sit in. At a minimum, give the person an opportunity to know what to expect. When you speak to that person's boss, make sure to have your facts together—times and dates of previous requests, and commitments made. And be succinct (again using your non-blaming, it-must-have-been-a-mistake tone).

He's Lost His Mind
Understand that everybody isn't going to operate like you do.

Appendix 10 is dedicated to explaining more in detail how to deal with differences of opinion and disagreements at work. So for now we'll just cover the basics. Understand the fact that everybody doesn't think like you. Understand this fact may result in disagreements. As in any relationship, because people are different, and see things from different points of view there are just times that are going to be tense and difficult. The tense and difficult discussions that come from trying to meet goals, share differences of opinion or opposing viewpoints, and resolving conflicts will exist within your co-worker group and at times with your boss or even at the executive level. You *must* handle these situations professionally.

Yes? No? Or *What?*
Disagreements: Stop and consider.

Disagreements are common, but it matters very much that they be handled respectfully—always. In the workplace, disagreements are usually about *what* needs to be done and/or *how* something should be done. When disagreeing with teammates, counterparts, resource or support people, to disagree for the sake of proving your point is a waste of time. If there's a chance for understanding so that business issues can be resolved, or to clarify something that will be helpful or useful, work it out. Listen to the other person with full attention.

The Best of Times, the Worst of Times—If you are trying to determine ways to meet shared goals, whether with teammates, counterparts, resource or support people, other managers or directors, executives or your boss, you'll want to use the "I'm open to hearing your ideas" tone. When your idea differs, share that difference but at the same time acknowledge the other person's thoughts as important. Everyone (including you) has an agenda and goals to meet. The way you go about meeting those goals may conflict with someone else on the team or in the company. If you can remember that ultimately you should all have the same goal—the success of the company—focusing on ways to meet goals becomes more important than the challenge of a disagreement. Work hard to understand what's important to the company, and find a way to meet both your goal and the other person's.

Members Only—With teammates, counterparts, resource or support people, you may have differences of opinion or opposing viewpoints that result in what may feel like a disagreement or argument. The way you express yourself during this type of exchange should be with a friendly tone, or at least one of curiosity and intrigue. Share your point of view, but at the same time acknowledge the other person's thoughts as valid. There's no need to have a challenging tone just to prove your point. To highlight your perspective without shouting, allow the other person to make his point and say, "Interesting the way you came up with that. Hmm, the way I see it is. . . ."

The Higher Ups—With executives or your boss, differences of opinion or viewpoints should be handled extremely carefully. Share your viewpoint in the most non-threatening way possible—the way you might give directions. You aren't concerned with making an executive or your boss wrong, you're simply introducing your perspective for the sake of introducing—not changing their minds. To an executive, submit your viewpoint only if asked. If the executive asks you specifically what you think about something, again, in the most non-threatening way possible, give your feedback. And remember to use a phrase like, "To *add* to *your thoughts,* extending the breaks from one to two o'clock would seem to help us be more refreshed, and more productive. . . ." If your perspective is not solicited, refrain from offering it.

Regarding executives (and their assistants), do your best to avoid disagreements altogether. If you feel otherwise, consult your boss for advice.

For further details on disagreeing with your co-worker group, refer also to Appendix 10.

But Boss, You Don't Understand
Disagreements with the boss: Do stop and consider.

Think carefully before disagreeing with him. There's a good chance you may have different opinions about policies, sales territories, compensation, promotions, raises, business decisions, and a host of other issues. Yet the way you express your thoughts is key. First you'll want to avoid disagreeing with your boss in a challenging tone. Instead of saying, "I don't agree," or "That's not right," or "No, you're wrong," you might say, "Help me understand what you mean by. . . ." This way you gain more information about his thoughts and also maintain a non-challenging tone.

Yuck!

Realize that complaining to your boss is another form of disagreement.

Complaining about work issues without having a solution is really just whining. Whining is usually a result of feeling like a victim. A victim usually believes he is helpless to do anything to change his circumstances. If you tend to complain, take your complaining to the next level of empowerment. Either think of a solution and try to influence a change, or choose to accept the situation and decide to make the best of the circumstances until you find a better way.

So, when you say to the boss that you don't like a policy that he put in place (complaining), in essence you're disagreeing with his decision. Be careful here. Though you may feel you're simply expressing your opinion, he most likely hears that you don't agree with him. Let's say something does come up that doesn't settle well with you. What do you do? Well, before voicing an opinion that's obviously different from his, stop and ask yourself a couple of questions. What exactly are you in disagreement about? What do you want instead? Is his decision or your request for change going to positively impact business results and the team as a whole? Depending upon your answer to those questions, you might also ask yourself if there is a better way to communicate your concern without coming across as challenging his decision. If you choose to complain, have a solution ready to present. State the solution's overall benefits and ask for consideration. Then leave it alone and wait for your answer.

Need an Example? Let's say you believe your opportunity for success is too limited and that opportunity is unfairly distributed among the team. First, make sure you have facts that support your claim, and outline the discrepancies. You may need to muster revenue reports (past and present), performance histories, records of past issues and concerns (documented if possible), and the like as evidence. Simply talking about the issues is not going to help. No evidence, no chance.

Second, have a clear understanding of what you want. Do you want a change in assignment? Do you need a temp to help with getting things organized? Do you need a typist? Several training classes? Do you need special computer software? Do you want additional resources? Do you want an adjustment to what's being asked of you? Or—do you want to point out why you're going to fail and why someone else is going to succeed? (Hint: the last option is *not* what you want.) Your goal is to demonstrate your ability to be successful, your commitment, and your ability to be a team player. You're not in this to compare yourself to teammates—the assumption is there is no comparison.

Lastly, be prepared to show your boss why you believe what you believe, gain his feedback to see if he sees what you see. If he does, gain his commitment to help you meet your goals, which are ultimately going to impact him. If he does not see what you do, ask him to elaborate on his perspective. Listen carefully to his feedback. Ask him if his perspective will prevent him from helping you meet your own goals. If so, ask him to tell you what he needs in order to change his mind. Write down the information, repeat his points aloud to confirm understanding, and ask for examples if necessary. Establish a timeframe to get what he needs and make a commitment to resolve the issue based on what he needs. Follow up this meeting with an email that summarizes the issues, your feedback, his request and commitment and the next meeting date.

This may sound like a lot of work. However, depending upon your agenda and how important it is to your overall success it may be very worthwhile. Do whatever you have to and get what you need—in the most professional way you can.

Don't Go There
Think carefully about disagreeing with the boss on touchy issues.

Before disagreeing with your boss on touchy issues, like whether or not you believe he made a good decision, again you must stop and think. Ask yourself whether what you're disagreeing about is anything your opinion can change. For example, if your boss has determined the way he wants to re-structure the team, and he neither asked for anyone's input nor made new assignments optional, leave it alone. The response you need to make is one that supports his decision, like it or not. And, no talking to others about your "real" feelings. There's a reason he's the boss and you're not. If your boss invites your opinion on a touchy issue, such as changing the pay structure—that's different. Even so, avoid alluding to the fact that you think his idea is wrong. Offer your opinion this way: "I can appreciate your vision. To build on your ideas, these are my thoughts. . . ."

Because He Said So
Avoid disagreeing with your boss over something he's asked you to do.

Lastly, minus anything immoral, illegal, or disrespectful, disagreeing with the boss about whether or not you're going to do what he asks you to do is altogether different. One caution: Consider the word "insubordination." For starters, insubordinate behavior is behavior that's considered unruly, disorderly, or defiant. Body language, tone of voice, and facial expressions can also be interpreted as insubordinate behavior. And whether your boss feels you are insubordinate is really his call, not yours. In essence, unless you are putting yourself in physical, emotional, spiritual, or mental harm, you're most likely going to have to comply with the boss's requests.

If you're disagreeing about how to handle a situation that falls within your job description, something he's entrusted you to be able to handle, be open to hearing his ideas. At least give him the benefit of the doubt that his experience is valuable. After you've listened, and you still feel your way is best, in the most humble but firm tone (because you want to show confidence without seeming confrontational or challenging), let him know that you would only do what's right for all involved.

You could say, "Your feedback is helpful. Let me share my thoughts as to why I've decided to do it this way. Based on my values, the company's goals, and your guidance, I believe the right thing to do is XXX. Your ideas are valuable. If it turns out that my decision was not best, I'll accept that responsibility and do what's needed to rectify the situation. Do I have your support?" If he says no, then honor his request and ask him to send you an email as to how he would like you to proceed. Keep a copy and file it in case the situation comes up and you need to refer back to the instruction you were given.

Nipped in the Bud
Do stand up for yourself.

If you disagree with the way your boss (or anyone, really) may have spoken to you, with something he's done to embarrass you, or with his failure to support you, then you have every reason to sit down and talk it over. Have a discussion about your beliefs, which are obviously different than his. These types of conversations are best to have face-to-face and, if possible, away from the office. If there's no time to go off the premises, find a private place to talk. Remember stay calm and simply restate the facts—what was actually said and done. If you maintain this approach, you'll probably be less defensive and more capable of remembering the facts. Your boss will likely be less defensive as well.

Approach the situation as if he simply made a mistake or didn't realize what he actually said or did could have been offensive to you. When your approach suggests that you're trying to clarify an *unintentional* mistake, you will be perceived as being open to hearing his explanation without judgment. And be ready to move forward. Remember to avoid disagreeing with the boss in an open setting like a team meeting, or anywhere where there's another person besides the two of you.

For further details on disagreeing with your boss, refer to Appendix 10.

> **Sports Talk**—*When the referee makes a bad call, rather than assuming he doesn't like you or he's an idiot, consider that he didn't have a clear view of what happened. Before you scream and jump in his face, consider the possibility that someone was standing in his way— he just didn't see the whole picture.*

Be Sure to Wear Your Mouthpiece

You realize conflicts are part of the workplace—so deal with them effectively.

In the course of doing business, struggles, clashes, encounters and confrontations can arise from simple misunderstandings, personality differences or disagreements within your co-worker group or with your boss. These situations are usually temporary (lasting from a few minutes to a few days), and once new information is presented, everyone seems to move on. Sometimes situations can turn into a conflict that's of a prolonged nature, such as the customer service department having an on-going battle with sales concerning when to refer customers to their 800 line. There are other situations that can turn into verbal attacks and even physical encounters (let's hope this doesn't happen with you). For the sake of clarification, I'm *not* referring to the latter. When I say conflicts, I'm not talking about physical brawls, or when you choose to not work with a person, or you halt business for days and weeks because you're angry. I'm talking about ordinary conflicts.

Resolving conflicts and then moving on is considered part of any good workplace relationship. What do you do when you find yourself in a conflict? Remain calm. Keep your voice lower than usual (this helps to relax you). Clarify the misunderstanding, introduce new information, be respectful. Ideally, there's a win-win—you win and the other person wins.

What *Did* You Mean?
Discuss conflicts in person (on the phone or face-to-face).

When you're trying to resolve conflicts that result from missed deadlines, miscommunication, or misunderstandings, using voicemail or email is risky (sending professional, unemotional messages takes practice). I suggest *not* leaving your viewpoint on a voicemail recording or in an email message—when sent, both are irreversible. It's best to pick up the phone and talk in person, or have a face-to-face visit. You might leave a person a voicemail message recommending that you get together to discuss your concerns. Ask what would be a good time to meet and leave your call-back number. And since the tone in emails can be easily misread, again, I don't advise disagreeing over email. Send an email requesting to talk.

Extra! Extra! Read All About It
If you find yourself in the middle of a misunderstanding or an issue that bothers you, involve as few people as possible.

If a situation arises, keep the issue between those directly involved. People in the office don't need to know that you "took care of a person." The perception you want is that you maintain professional working relationships even when faced with conflicts. If you want ideas as to what to do, discuss the situation with people who don't work at the same company and who are at least in a position above yours (if you're an entry level salesman, talk to someone who is perhaps a manager, director, or higher).

It Really Doesn't Matter Anyway
Avoid taking things personally.

In general, if someone does or says something to you that feels like a personal attack, and even if it is, try not to receive it as a personal attack. However, address the offense quickly so as not to let a potential misunderstanding go unresolved too long. If someone says something you feel is inappropriate you could say in a calm tone (thinking in your mind that the comment *must have been* a mistake), "Share with me what you meant by. . . ." Usually, the person will realize their mistake and try to explain that they meant no harm. In this case, make a mental note that the person has issues you may not know about. Move on in peace.

Nah, That Wasn't Right—When an insulting or derogatory comment is said to you when no one else is present, or in front of one or more people, once again you should handle it as you did in the above scenario. Just be sure your face and body language don't reveal anger or confrontation. You already know who you are—this is not the time to forget.

It's *Not* Your Thing
Realize, people change when they get ready.

When a co-worker does something to you that really upsets you (like being rude, negative or catty), know that neither you, nor your anger, nor your setting them straight, nor your ignoring them, nor your getting revenge will heal this person or his "issues." This may not be someone you can share personal information with, or this may not be someone you can share all your work strategies with.

Turning the Tide—When people make comments to try and make you look bad, what do you do? Remember that you are not the one with the issue—they are. Remember there are people who like to highlight the faults of others because they don't feel so sure about themselves. And remember too that there are also people who will put you down in order to feel they are better than you.

Let's say you really did make a mistake. No problem. Everyone does. You're in good company. Yet if someone makes a comment to purposely spotlight your mistake (openly or between the two of you), in that calm, confident tone, you could say something like this: "I've corrected the situation and I'm moving forward with the solution. Is there additional feedback you'd like to offer as we move forward?" If someone tries to shift unwarranted blame to you or otherwise make you look bad, and you know you've covered all your bases and you didn't make a mistake, you might say something like this: "Based on the information I was provided, I offered the following. . . . Was there more that I wasn't made aware of?"

My Personal Notes

Take a few minutes and make note of any information that stood out:

_____

_____

_____

_____

_____

_____

_____

_____

What will you do differently as a result of what you've read?

_____

_____

_____

_____

_____

_____

_____

_____

Off-Season | Before It's All Over, It Begins Again

You've spent a great deal of time making sure your outer appearance is correct and your workspace organized. You're utilizing resources and tools to be productive and respecting company privileges. You're clear about your role on the team. You're relating with your boss and co-workers appropriately, achieving high performance results, socializing professionally, and making positive contributions to the company. At this point, you should be well prepared and applying the fundamentals of the game—keeping in mind that everything you do builds a certain perception and can become your foundation for success.

So you're in the off-season. What do I mean? This is not a time when you're off (after work hours, vacation or leave of absence) but rather a point in your career in which you're moving out of the new-hire role and into a more settled and established role as a tenured employee. This is a period in your career in which you begin to develop and execute the game plan for your future at the company—professionally, financially, and personally. In the off-season work to stay in shape.

There are a host of ways to fine-tune your game—talking with confidantes, personal champions, and mentors, pursuing higher education, understanding investment options, and celebrating successes, just to name a few. While the pace of the game has slowed, you've still got to focus on staying fit. There is much to do. Keep in mind that success is a process not a destination.

And after this section, to encourage you in your process, the book closes with motivational quotes from those who've made awesome contributions to the world.

On A Professional Tip

I'm O.K., You're O.K.
Find someone outside your company in which to confide.

The perception you want at work is that you have things together, and you do. Yet everyone needs to talk to someone about work-related difficulties from time to time. That's why it's a good idea to get the reinforcement and reassurance you need outside the office. When you need to talk things over to gain a new perspective, talk to a good friend who doesn't work for the same company, maybe one who doesn't live in the same city or state.

You Should Check Him Out . . .
Know your "personal champions."

"Personal champions" are not necessarily mentors or people you spend a great deal of time with. Generally personal champions are people who work at the same company and are above you in title, those who sense your potential, respect your work, and know that you are well perceived and successful. These people will say positive things about you and hold your abilities up for everyone to see. When asked if they know a person that would be a good candidate for a particular job or assignment, they offer your name.

This relationship is natural, and you won't necessarily work closely with them. You won't necessarily ask a person to be your personal champion, rather, you just kind of listen for people who openly compliment your work, put your name among top performers, and so forth. It's important to know who they are so you're always showing them your best.

Going back to what I said earlier about building perceptions of yourself as professional, intelligent, and skillful—these qualities become key to attracting personal champions. Having several such champions from different areas of the company is also helpful—both in and outside of your department is ideal.

Wise and Trusted One

Consider a mentor.

A mentoring relationship usually happens once you've established a solid professional foundation as a new hire (consistently applying the things we've discussed in earlier chapters). What a mentor does and the role he plays in your corporate life can sometimes be unclear. So let's take a closer look.

A mentor is a person who provides insight and helps you to successfully navigate through the workplace. A mentor doesn't have to work for the same company as you, and can be male or female. A mentor influences you to make changes so you can improve aspects of your work—including personal development. A mentor is someone who takes an active and proactive role in helping you succeed. A mentor is someone who watches over you, looks out for your best interest in the workplace, and alerts you to consider new ways of doing things. A mentor is like a corporate God Parent. A mentor is like a coach that runs alongside you to encourage you, scold you, motivate you. You will have to spend time getting to know this person as he expresses an interest in getting to know you and helping you professionally. A mentor may verbally extend himself, or he may just be around to help without ever saying the words, "I'd like to help you."

A mentor is not just someone you admire, but someone with whom you can pick up the phone and talk, someone who doesn't mind being involved in your life. This person agrees to provide the one-on-one coaching you'll need, and that includes pushing you to go beyond your comfort zones. A mentor wants nothing in return except your success.

Whether it's formal mentoring, which some companies provide for new hires, or informal and unassigned, having a mentor generally makes a psychological difference. You will feel like you're a step ahead of the game. Those fortunate enough to have a mentor tend to be more confident in their decisions, gain more knowledge quicker, and get more career-related support overall.

Developing a mentoring relationship can be a difficult task. But if you develop a trusting relationship with someone who fits the description of a mentor, it might naturally begin to include advice, regular meetings, consultations, and so on.

As you see, being a mentor is a rather large responsibility— probably why they're tough to find.

To find out more about mentors and how to get one, refer to the book listed in Appendix 11.

Higher Learning 101
Continue your education.

Whatever your field, look for opportunities to continue your education. Consider everything from non-degree classes all the way to master's and doctoral degrees—it can all be incredibly helpful. Continue to develop yourself. You'll be even more marketable in the job arena. For example, graduate coursework in business gives you a broader understanding of the world of business: systems, policies, currencies, human relations, and much more. A master's or doctorate degree tend to make you more eligible for promotions and higher salaries.

Habla Espanol?
Learn a foreign language and travel.

If the company doesn't offer it as a class, on your own time, learn a foreign language, and if you have the opportunity, offer to take an international assignment. "Global this" and "global that" are standard jargon these days. A graduate degree in international policy, international business, or international anything seems pretty practical. International assignments are particularly valued at industrial manufacturing companies. If you have no interest in international experiences to build your resume, it's still a good idea to travel as much as possible and learn as much about various cultures as you can.

The Green Stuff

Learn to play golf.

If your job is one that involves building relationships with clients for sales or marketing purposes, consider learning to play golf. The time you share on the golf course allows you to build key business relationships. If you are going to play, understand how to use the time with a client to your advantage. And remember to invite female clients to play as well.

First of all, learn the rules including golf etiquette. Decide who to join as golf partners—stick with decision-makers, or at least people you will get the most business from. Figure out what you want to accomplish or walk away with (a sales order, hidden objections, etc.).

Begin talking about topics other than business. And plan to finish any business discussions before the last few holes. Again, I recommend avoiding alcohol, but if you decide to drink, limit your consumption. The golf course is not the place to embarrass yourself.

Whatever your profession, learning to play this game will no doubt lend to your ability to build relationships you may not otherwise have a chance to. Use the time to learn more about your customers, relate to them on a personal level and simply get to know them better. It's a funny thing—people who don't have time to see you in the office somehow can manage to spend hours with you on the golf course.

Remember you're always creating a perception, even on the golf course. If your game is in need, keep taking lessons until you are able to grasp and execute the basics. According to golf etiquette, if your game is more advanced than your customer's, do not purposely let your client win. Rather, use the time to help him with certain parts of his game. Apparently people correlate the way you help them or treat them when they're in trouble on the golf course with the way you would treat them should they need assistance with a business solution you've proposed. If you're trying to fool a bad player into thinking he beat you, he may become suspicious of your business tactics as well. Play honestly. There are companies that offer seminars. So remember to take a course in golf protocol—no pun intended—of *course*.

On a Financial Tip

Your Bait and Tackle Shop
Invest in the company's 401K or retirement program.

Review your employee investment and retirement options. If you're interested in saving money for a house, for your child's education, or simply for retirement, you might elect to have a percentage of your income withdrawn from your check. Not only do you save money for retirement you'll learn better how to manage on a smaller salary. There are various avenues available to you, so take advantage of them. Financial investments outside the company are also a good idea.

On a Personal Tip

Continuous Improvement
Focus on personal development.

Continue to attend as many seminars, workshops, and conferences as possible. From personal development to industry specifics, continue to learn and grow. Many companies provide a menu of education and development courses. Consider contacting your Training and Development Department or accessing your company's Intranet for a listing of available courses. And, if you want to keep up with what's going on in the world of work and fine-tune your career knowledge, visit career-related web sites.

For a list of web addresses, see Appendix 12.

Different Strokes for Different Folks
Join company-sanctioned groups dedicated to helping you.

Most companies try to provide a setting in which people can get together for a common cause and to improve themselves in some way (as long as it's not hindering company business). And so there may be specific groups within the company dedicated to assisting you in the workplace. It's a good idea to join and get involved. Such groups usually consist of people with common interests (male mentors), cultural backgrounds (a Jewish Association or African American Caucus), or goals (financial club). Groups like this generally meet after office hours to provide various levels of support and mentoring.

You Are the Reason
Take a moment to feel good about your accomplishments and maintain balance.

When you accomplish your goals for the day, or when you complete an important task, be content to consider that you've done a great job for that day. Give yourself a mental party. Celebrate. Sometimes it takes practice to really allow yourself to experience the good feelings that come from accomplishing a task.

The pace of business doesn't always allow for long celebrations, but you can recognize your own achievement in smaller ways. You could treat yourself to a great lunch, and even buy balloons and tie them to the back of your chair (as long as the balloons aren't distracting to clients). You could also treat yourself to your favorite CD, take an evening jog or bike-ride and enjoy the scenery. You could go to the arcade and play as many games as you want. You could simply pat yourself on the back and say, "Outstanding!" Whatever you do, find a way to celebrate your accomplishments.

New Balance—The key to spiritual, physical, emotional, and mental health is balance. If you make a habit of working hours far beyond your body's physical and mental well-being, not only will your friends write you off, you'll burn out way too early in your career. There may be times when work calls for extra hours and weekends, but try not to make a habit of that pace. Learn ways to use your time effectively while you're at work so that you can take time to rest, build personal relationships, and simply feel good about life. Balance is key in all you do.

Free Agency

I'm Outta' Here
Understand your value, but remember you're replaceable.

Don't overestimate your value. For the most part, the moment you announce your decision to resign your position, your boss, co-workers, and staff will miss you—for a few minutes. After that, the race is on. Strategy sessions are held to determine who will replace you. Don't be surprised at questions like, "When can you brief so and so?"

> **Sports Talk**—*It's like getting hurt during the championship game. The coach races onto the floor to make sure you're not dead. Then, without taking a breath, he looks down the bench and in three seconds he decides who's going to take your spot.*

And . . . depending upon the circumstances of your resignation, be ready for a number of responses. If you're leaving to work for another company (a competitor), don't be surprised if you're immediately asked to leave and even escorted to the door. If you're leaving the company to work for a company that isn't considered competition, you might be allowed to stay through the duration of your resignation date. If you're leaving your position but staying with the company locally but moving to a different department, you might be asked to help select and even train the person coming into your position. You might even be called on for information long after you're in your next position. If you're relocating or simply resigning for other reasons, you're usually allowed to work through your last day. Whatever the case, think about the terms of your departure and anticipate the reactions so you can prepare yourself.

Tidy Up
If you're leaving, make copies of what you need and review your files with your boss.

If there are personal items you wish to take with you (not including the company's property—and you may want to carefully read the employee handbook to confirm what the company considers it's property) take them before you announce your plans to leave. Even if you're not going to work for a company that's considered a competitor, you may not have as much time to pack as you would like. I don't mean pack boxes and load them into your car every day for a week before you announce your resignation. Simply gather the things that are yours little by little so that it's not noticeable that you're planning to leave. Make sure to keep your performance reviews, awards, plaques, and certificates of achievement. Although there's a copy somewhere of all the work you've done on your laptop or computer, you might want to review and delete things that are no longer useful. Pick up the latest edition of the corporate directory, annual report, and organization chart.

Bye-Bye—Once your announcement is made, say good-bye to your customers and, if possible, ask them to write letters of recommendation. Resolve any hard feelings or misunderstandings with co-workers before you leave. You never know when you'll cross paths again. And one day you may even want to return to the job you're leaving. Collect business cards from your co-workers, managers, etc. (once you leave, you quickly forget those commonly dialed extensions, email addresses and even office addresses). The company you once worked for may be a potential client in your new ventures.

No Hangnails—Provided you are not immediately dismissed you might sit down with your boss and review any unfinished business and give him a list of things to complete. Close any outstanding business issues. This is extremely beneficial for your boss. Be sure to depart on the best possible terms. *Once again, you never know when you may wish to seek re-employment.*

Finally, to your next venture, take with you everything you've learned about building perceptions and foundations for success as a new hire—they'll help you get off to a good start.

Best wishes, and remember: *before it's all over, it begins . . . again.*

My Personal Notes

Take a few minutes and make note of any information that stood out:

_____

_____

_____

_____

_____

_____

_____

_____

What will you do differently as a result of what you've read?

_____

_____

_____

_____

_____

_____

_____

_____

From the Coaching Staff |
Business Advice

"There's no substitute for confidence. You can have all the talent in the world, but if you don't believe it, it doesn't mean anything in this business."
Robert Parish, former NBA player

"Leadership is not about knowledge, about being the smartest. It's about results."
Jack Zenger, author and chair, Times Mirror Training, Inc., the world's largest group of employee training companies

"You have to expect things of yourself before you can do them."
Michael Jordan, former NBA player, one of the fifty greatest players in the history of the NBA

"It is at the bottom of life we must begin, and not at the top. Nor should we permit our grievances to overshadow our opportunities."
Booker T. Washington (1815-1915), born into slavery, self-educated, founder and first president of Tuskegee Institute in Alabama

"Beware the naked man who offers you his shirt."
Harvey Mackay, author and business consultant

"It's better to be prepared for an opportunity and not have one than to have an opportunity and not be prepared."
Whitney Young (1921-1971), author and former executive director of the National Urban League

"That which you think about expands. Therefore, develop the habit of always focusing on what you want, not what you don't want."
Wayne Dyer, psychologist, motivational speaker, and author

"There's no need to overpower when you can out-smart."
Phil Jackson, author and head coach, NBA

"A problem is a chance for you to do your best."
Duke Ellington (1899-1974), legendary jazz musician, composer, and bandleader

"In your moments of challenge, you will need a vision of how . . . to go above and beyond."
Pat Riley, NBA coach

"Every problem does not need to be solved."
Michael Owens, financial analyst, Eli Lilly Company

"All you have left after a crisis is your conduct during it."
Johnnie Cochran, author, trial lawyer, and co-founder of the law firm Cochran, Mitchell & Lotkin

"Experience is not what happens to a man; it's what a man does with what happens to him."
Aldous Huxley (1894-1963), author

"Put that smile on your face and keep living."
Magic Johnson, businessman and former NBA player—named one of the fifty greatest players in the history of the NBA

"You don't just get a work ethic, you've got to come with it."
Karl Malone, businessman and NBA player—named one of the fifty greatest players in the history of the NBA

"To be good at anything—be it in sports, school or being somebody's friend—it takes a great deal of work, concentration and sacrifice."
Walter Payton (1954-1999), businessman, and former NFL player—set NFL rushing record, elected to the Pro Football Hall of Fame, 1993

"Part of networking is learning how to get into the system as well as learning what kind of skills are needed."
Alvin Poussaint, professor of psychiatry, Harvard University Medical School

"When you suffer something like that defeat . . . one of two things is going to happen. You are going to learn from that experience or you're going to crumble beneath the memory. We had the right kind of character to not give up. [That] prepared us to be champions."
Joe Dumars, former NBA player

"Even if you are on the right track, you'll get run over if you just sit there."
Will Rogers (1879-1935), actor

"Before you run, check to see if the bulldog has teeth."
Les Brown, motivational speaker and author

"In a moment of decision, the best thing you can do is the right thing to do. The worst thing you can do is nothing."
Theodore Roosevelt (1858-1919), twenty-sixth U.S. president

"To be a great champion you must believe you are the best. If you're not, pretend you are."
Muhammad Ali, 10-time world heavy-weight boxing champion

"The majority of people in the world don't do what it takes to win. Everyone is looking for the easy road."
Charles Barkley, former professional basketball player, NBA MVP, 1992

"If you can somehow think and dream of success in small steps, every time you make a step, every time you accomplish a small goal, it gives you confidence to go on from there."
John H. Johnson, publisher (*Negro Digest* and *Ebony* magazine), consumer products executive, and founder, Johnson Publishing Co.

"Life has two rules: Number 1, Never quit!; Number 2, Always remember rule Number 1."
Duke Ellington (1899-1974), legendary jazz musician, composer and bandleader

Appendix 1 | Preparing For Employment

The purpose of this appendix is not necessarily to prepare you for job interviews. It's simply to help you remember important considerations when it comes to choosing a work environment that is best suited for your personality so there's a better fit between you and the company. Even if you omit some of these steps, the information is still helpful. So with these things in mind, take seriously what it means to . . .

Decide the position you want.

Let's say you want to be a corporate professional. Let's say you enjoy persuading people to make decisions, you're an overachiever and want to be recognized by the work you do. You're comfortable with meeting a monthly quota and being paid on sales. You are the type of person who enjoys risk in your job and being primarily responsible to make as much money as you believe you can. Let's say you're a self-starter who thrives on challenges. Perhaps you'll consider a sales position.

You'll want to determine what portion of your pay is based on salary and what portion is based on commissions. You'll also want to know about the pay plan—is there a maximum dollar amount you can reach? Is there unlimited money that can be made? Are there bonuses? And if so, how often can you earn them? Are there special incentives?

Research the industry.

First, understand the difference between an industry and a corporation. The industry is the overall chosen field of specialized products or profession of specialized services. Corporations—or companies—make up the industry and produce the goods or services. AT&T is a corporation, telecommunications is the industry.

Learn all you can about the industry you're interested in working in. Go to a library and read the industry magazines. Surf the Internet. Talk to people in the industry. Try to find out what's going on in the industry—trends and changes.

Assessing the industry helps you decide how well you are suited for a particular field and gives you an idea of what to expect. Before I accepted a sales position in wireless telecommunications—I researched the wireless telecommunications industry. I found that at that time, wireless telecommunications was considered a young, fast-paced industry. Technology was advancing very quickly and new competitors were on the horizon.

The corporation where I work is part of an industry that requires constant change—as a result I had to change the way I did business too. Over the years I learned to expect, sometimes daily, new rules, new business processes, new customer requirements, and new business solutions. I had to expect new technology that would sometimes become old within a month of being announced. Add mergers to the equation and it made the industry much like the stock market. As a matter of fact, the company has recently completed a joint venture with two other companies, and will soon be completing a merger with another. Since I've worked there the name has changed three or four times already! Today it's called Verizon Wireless, formerly Bell Atlantic Mobile.

Determine an industry and personality match.

Consider the atmosphere—ever changing trends and new technology coming faster and faster—and decide you're ready, willing, and able to handle the ride. Be honest with yourself, this is very important for your peace of mind and your values. If you work best in an environment where the way business is conducted is well defined and process-oriented, because business processes tend to change rapidly, a profession in the wireless telecommunications industry for example may not be the best fit. These days, most industries are in some state of change. But the difference might be the pace of that change. The atmosphere can be more or less relaxed depending on the company and the resources they have in place to support such change.

Select and research the corporation.

Knowing the company goals and objectives, and where they're positioned in the industry helps you decide how you feel about working for them. You might want to work for a corporation that is leading the industry, or you may be challenged by the thought of helping a company gain a number one or two position within their industry. There's really no right or wrong approach. It's whatever's best for you.

Basically, use the same approach you did with the industry research—library, Internet, people. Start with the company's annual report most readily found on their web site on the Internet. You might also obtain a copy from their office lobby or by contacting their Corporate Communications department. Additional information can also be found in library reference books such as, *The Career Guide, Dun's Employment Opportunities Directory, Moody's Manuals* and *Standard & Poor's Register of Corporations, Directors and Executives. Appendix 12 offers additional web addresses to help with your research.*

Consider the size of an organization. Size may affect the company's decision-making policies—easy or difficult, short or long, bearable or unbearable. The size of a company may also determine the type of exposure that exists. For example, a smaller company may provide greater and/or faster opportunities for advancement: fewer layers, more direct access to departmental, regional, and corporate decision-makers, more potential to be personally noticed. The size of a company may also impact earnings potential, benefits, stock options, retirement plans, and extra benefits such as tuition assistance or childcare.

Kevin left a large corporation to work for a much smaller company. One day he received a call from someone on the legal staff—they were following up on a contract he'd submitted. Initially, Kevin was nervous about being personally contacted. He later realized that receiving follow-up calls from the legal staff was a standard procedure—something he never experienced at his former job.

At a smaller company, exposure at high levels can open doors of opportunity faster than normal, as long as you handle yourself professionally. At a larger corporation, there's a chance you'll be so far removed that it could be a long time before you ever meet anyone in the legal department. This doesn't mean you won't have an opportunity at a larger corporation. You may have to be more focused on performing well and networking to get your name mentioned to the right people who can talk about you to the other right people and so forth. The point is, decide what size company fits you best.

Study the corporate culture.

Corporate culture is simply a particular way of doing things—the types of behaviors a company fosters. More formally, corporate culture represents a system of shared values and beliefs. It reflects what a company perceives to be important—how it does things, what it does and does not do.

When I was employed at Xerox, I was introduced to the corporate belief that selling products required more than brochure knowledge. Part of the corporate culture was a belief in quality that extended to every part of the business. Every sales representative spent weeks, sometimes months, learning first-hand about the products we sold.

Corporate identity, reflected in such things as logos and building structures, can also help you determine what a company believes and thinks. Incentives and rewards—recognition for providing excellent business solutions—also reflect a company's culture. If possible, visit the company. Some companies allow visitors to tour the building. Once inside, observe. Are there motivational materials hanging on the walls? Are the company's value-statements visible? Are there performance and goal charts hanging up? Are there "job well done" plaques or balloons? Do you feel a sense of teamwork and celebration in the air?

Cultural diversity is another factor defining corporate culture. Your research should help determine how diverse the company is. The annual report may even have pictures that reflect diversity. If you visit the company notice the various cultures represented.

Many elements shape a company's culture. Remember that corporate culture often takes years to evolve, so if you don't like what you see but you think you are going to go in and change things overnight, you may want to reconsider.

If visits to a company are not possible, maybe there's a corporate professional you can talk to where you worship or in your community. If you know that person well, you might ask him to allow you to visit him at work so you can observe the setting. If you're still in college, you might also ask your career counselor if he could arrange a visit. And finally, read books detailing people's first-hand experience at a particular corporation.

The point is, do whatever you have to and find out what you need to know—the more you know, the more prepared you are to make the best decisions about where you want to work and for whom.

Assess your personality and abilities.

Personality—Are you shy or outgoing? Do you like challenges? Are you a risk taker? Do you learn by reading, hearing or doing? Do you enjoy meeting new people? Are you self-motivated? Do you respond well to change? Do you prefer supervision or working alone? Do you enjoy being in the spotlight or behind the scenes?

Environment—Do you prefer to be indoors or outdoors? Do you like working on a team or by yourself? Do you prefer an office workplace or home office? Do you prefer large cafeterias or a small designated lunch area? Do you prefer an office workout facility?

Gifts and Abilities—Are you a writer or speaker? Are you organized or unorganized? Are you detail-oriented or do you mainly see the big picture? Are you a visionary? Are you task-oriented? Are you a dreamer? Are you a doer? Are you a leader or a follower? Are you creative, analytical, or technical? Are you an innovator? If you aren't aware of these details, try completing a personality assessment test—it's a great self-discovery tool.

Determine company and personality match.

Depending on the importance, try to match your overall needs with a company you believe will help motivate you to reach your potential at work. Don't feel pressured to pick the right industry and the perfect corporation. Sometimes, no matter how much research you do, it's difficult to know how things will work out. If you have an opportunity, test the waters—try a temporary or part-time job, work a few months, and see how you like it.

A note to those currently in jobs but thinking of leaving—if you're unfulfilled at work, before you resign, consider applying for a different position in another area within the company. You might be a customer service representative, but outside sales would fit you best. If you find yourself wanting to do something other than what you're doing, at an entirely different company, in an entirely different industry, then plan, prepare, and go for it.

Appendix 2 | Goal Setting Exercise

Goal setting can be as simple as deciding what you're having for dinner, or as complex as mapping out what you want to do with the rest of your life (relationally, professionally, spiritually, financially, educationally, recreationally, and so on).

To begin mapping out your goals, use the following worksheet I've adapted from a book called, What Are Your Goals: Powerful Questions to Discover What You Want Out of Life, by Gary Ryan Blair.

My Goals

Date:
Category (Personal, Financial, Educational, etc.):
Goal:

Goal Statement: Example: I pay off my car by October 31st.

_____

_____

_____

_____ short-range (1-90 days)
_____ mid-range (3-12 months)
_____ long-range (1-5 years)

Why do I want to do this? What are the benefits? (Prioritize them.)
1._____
2._____
3._____
4._____
5._____

Where am I starting from right now?

_____

_____

_____

What are the risks? (real/imagined)

_____

_____

_____

What are the obstacles?

_____

_____

_____

What do I have to sacrifice or invest?

_____

_____

_____

What additional knowledge do I need?

_____

_____

_____

Who do I need help from to achieve this goal?

_____

_____

_____

Develop a plan . . .

Priority	Activity	Target Date	Date Completed
_____	_____	_____	_____
_____	_____	_____	_____
_____	_____	_____	_____
_____	_____	_____	_____
_____	_____	_____	_____

Set a deadline . . .
(What date will you achieve this goal?)

_____

I will reward myself by:

_____

_____

_____

Appendix 3 | Goal Setting
Encouragement

You can do it! Decide on your goal, then go, go, go!
Take one step today to help you reach your goal—then let the first
step energize your second, the second your third, the third your
fourth. . . . And, to get you in the mood for goal setting, here are a
few words from motivational speaker Brian Tracy*:

"Ideas are a dime a dozen but the person who puts
them into practice can be worth a million."

"Set a goal. Stay with it until it's met."

"Any new venture seems uphill and the wind's in
your face. Press on!"

*Quotations are from an audiovisual shown at a business
conference in 1999 entitled, "The Phoenix Seminar for Maxi-
mum Achievement," hosted by Diane Muntean, President,
Peak Performance, Inc.

Ready? Set. *Goal*?!*

If you tend to get as far as writing out your goals, but end up frustrated because, as hard as you try, you can't seem to actually accomplish your goals, hang in there. Setting goals might be relatively easy—accomplishing them can be challenging. If this is you (you'll know from the tiny elbow poking you in the side right now), take a time-out and complete the exercise below. You'll find—as is often said, "Even eagles need a push."

Goal Setting Encouragement Exercise

What do I need to change my mind about as it relates to how to accomplish my goals? (i.e., thinking things like, "I can't do this." "It's too hard." "Why try?")

Current Thoughts:

_____

_____

_____

What new thoughts will I think?

_____

_____

_____

By When? _____

Did you accomplish your goal? _____ yes _____ no

What words am I speaking that might be hindering me from accomplishing my goals?

Current Words:

_____

_____

_____

What new words will I speak to help me accomplish my goals?

_____

_____

_____

By When? _____

Did you accomplish your goal? _____ yes _____ no

What do I need to start reading to help me accomplish my goals?

_____

_____

_____

By When? _____

Did you accomplish your goal? _____ yes _____ no

Names of Books/Magazines   Date Completed

_____   _____

_____   _____

_____   _____

_____   _____

What do I need to start listening to, to accomplish my goals?

_____

_____

_____

By When? _____

Did you accomplish your goal? _____ yes _____ no

Names of Recordings   Dates Listened to

_____   _____

_____   _____

_____   _____

_____   _____

Appendix 4 | Setting Perception Goals

Remember the definition of a goal. A goal is a place you'd like to end up. Steps (tasks, activities, etc.) get you to your goals. "By When's" get you there on time. Depending on the goal, it might be useful to add By When's to your steps (see second example).

Example #1

Desired Perception—To be perceived as timely to team meetings.
Desired Date—First team meeting, 1/15.

Steps/Tasks:

1. Mark dates and times in my planner.
2. Pre-arrange to leave home early for work.
3. Arrive 30 minutes before each meeting.
4. Stick my head in the boss's office, say, "Hi."
5. Ask boss if I can help with anything.
6. Sit in the meeting room 10 minutes early.
7. Bring donuts or bagels.

Additional Perception Goals:
Accurate, Decisive, Positive, Professional, Interested, Helpful, Intelligent, Informed, Committed, Honest, Fair, Flexible, Patient, Aware, Successful, Teachable, Adaptable, and even a Goal-Setter!

Example #2

Desired Perception—To be perceived as very informed.
Desired Date—4/1.

Steps/Tasks:
1. Read the daily newspapers. **By When?** Start 1/1.
2. Read industry magazines. **By When?** 1/2.
    *(If there are none in your office, subscribe, and keep the
    most recent issue on your desk).*
3. Share related articles at team meetings. **By when?** 1/15.
    (Assuming this is your next meeting).
4. Compile a competitive information binder. **By When?** Start
    2/1.

Appendix 5 | The Initial Meeting with Your Boss

Don't worry if you can't fit everything on the initial meeting list into one meeting. Depending on your job description and how talkative you and your boss are, this overall meeting could be lengthy and require several meetings to adequately cover each area.

Because the list is somewhat comprehensive, you may find it best to decide which elements you wish to discuss first and group them into sub—or mini-meetings. So, let's say you break your meetings up into 3 separate events.

Since you'll be taking notes and your boss may be referencing materials as well, the first time you get together you might meet in his office or a conference room. To set your boss's expectations, be clear about what you want to talk about, how much time you'll need, and what you need him to be prepared to provide. For example, you could say you would like to have a shared dialogue about your job description, your role on the team, his expectations, your expectations, and the best methods to contact him. You would tell him you'll need approximately 30-40 minutes, and that you'd like a hard copy of your job description. You'd mention that you'd like him to provide hard copies of the objectives for your position as well.

For the next meeting, you might schedule lunch (a more relaxed environment). You might not have to alert him as to the topics you want to discuss, you might just casually ask him to go out to lunch.

During the ride to the restaurant or during the walk down to the cafeteria, begin your conversation around the areas of empowerment and accountability, business and corporate goals. Lunch is a good time to ask a lot of questions and listen intently and share philosophies.

The next set of topics to discuss might be done in another meeting at the office. At this time, you'll go over the role of your teammates, take a look at the organizational chart, talk about policies and procedures, and even introduce your Action Plan.

Relationship building is an on-going task. If your boss tries to minimize the importance of your meetings by saying something like, "Oh, I don't feel it's necessary to meet unless there's a crisis," remember the information is important to you. So go ahead and schedule the meetings (you may have to talk about things one at a time in 10-15 minutes, you may have to get creative about how you have your discussion). Whatever you have to do, cover this information:

Job Description and Pay Plan

Discuss in detail the job elements and ask your boss to give you examples if you're unclear about any part of what he's saying. Find out what the job means to your boss and his interpretation of the elements. Take notes. This is your opportunity to gain a clear understanding of what you're to do. Ask for a clear set of objectives that you can measure. Whatever targets and goals are set for you, you'll want to ask your manager how he thinks you're to meet them, and how he will determine if you have met them. For example, let's say you're expected to answer a minimum of 50 customer calls each day. Then 50 calls becomes your daily target or objective. Whatever the target or goal, make sure it's an actual number or something you can quantify. "Fifty" is a clear target. "Answer as many as you can" is not.

Once you have your target, you'll want to ask if there's a form or tool to help you keep track of your progress and the steps you need to take to meet your target. If there isn't such a tool, make one yourself. Then you'll need to know how you will be measured for that target. In other words, you'll ask if 50 calls are the standard, and if anything above 50 is considered outstanding. Or is there a ranking—51-60 is rated great, 61-75 is stellar? You'll want to know if your peers have the same objectives. If they don't, ask why or why not. At this point, you're not trying to change what's established for your peers. You simply want to understand what your target means in relation to similar objectives.

You'll want to know the reward for each accomplishment. Is there a bonus after a particular goal is met?

Finally, you'll want all this information in hard copy, or otherwise documented. If he doesn't have the information ready in hard copy, ask your boss for a "By When" date and follow up until you receive the information. This comes in handy around appraisal time. For now, just be clear on what you're expected to do.

Pay Plan—Get a clear understanding when you're paid and if there are bonuses. This is also a time to schedule a meeting with Personnel so you can ask questions about employee benefits, vacation time, personal days, holiday schedules, and company retirement options. Generally much of this information is made available via the corporate Intranet or company newsletter. Nevertheless, it's always a good idea to personally meet with your Human Resource coordinator, review the details of your plan, and begin to develop a relationship.

Your Role

Ask what your specific role is on the team. Be clear about what's expected of you every day. What you're to do and "By When" are part of knowing what's expected of you.

Sports Talk—Players have different roles and positions, and in order for the team to win, everybody has to play his own position. If two people are playing the same position at the same time, they're going to bump into each other and look like they don't know what they're doing. For example, as the point guard, one of your objectives is to assist others in scoring points. You either feed the ball to the person driving down the lane or kick the ball out to the outside shooter. If you're a power forward, your objective is to do whatever it takes to get open so that the point guard has a clear passing lane to get you the ball. Knowing your position drives what you do.

Expectations—The Boss's and Yours

This should be a two-way discussion. You have expectations and so does your boss. The two of you need to have a candid discussion about what they are—generally and specifically. General expectations could include job arrival and departure times, how often you should meet individually, or response time on issues and questions. Specific expectations could include feedback about job performance like asking your boss what behaviors he expects from you, or what types of behaviors he considers outstanding. This is also the time to ask which meetings (besides team meetings and mandatory meetings) or activities are best for you to attend.

And be sure to identify the "deliverables." Deliverables are those things you're expected to bring to reality, to deliver, to contribute—*tangible* results. Once you assess your deliverables, be clear about what you'll need to accomplish them. If you discover you need to perform a task that requires a skill that may not be your strength, ask your boss for ways you might get additional insight. Avoid telling him you know nothing about the subject. Rather, suggest that to ensure you're as current as you can be, perhaps there's a class you could take. The class may be provided by the company, the company may sponsor your attendance or you might have to take the class on your own. You could also ask if the class could be expensed. Whatever the case, prepare yourself. If you're getting additional training, be sure to let your boss know the date you'll be taking the class. When you've completed the course, you might give him a verbal recap or written summary, just to remind him of the value of the class and your seriousness in being effective. In addition to the class, there's probably a book on the subject that's an excellent resource. Get the name of the book. Take the initiative to read the material and get yourself up to speed.

Contacting Your Boss

Find out how your boss prefers to be contacted. Ask him who you should contact for day to day business needs as well as for urgent matters when he's unavailable. Find out how he prefers to be updated, in writing or verbally, in person, or by voicemail. And be certain you know what your boss considers urgent.

Empowerment and Accountability

Ask your boss how he defines empowerment. Find out his position on empowerment, whether he supports it or not. If he does support it, ask him to give you examples of when he empowered himself and explain both the good and bad results. Ask what he learned. Ask the same about accountability.

Regardless of his philosophy on empowerment, find out what types of decisions your boss feels comfortable allowing you to make without asking him. Ask for examples. Ask what kinds of business decisions he would want you to pass by him first.

Sample questions:

- *"At what point in a situation do you want me to seek your help?"*
- *"Will you support me if I take a risk and fail?"*
- *"When is a status report necessary?"*

Business Goals—The Boss's and Yours

Find out what's important to your boss. Uncover what he's trying to accomplish. Know his key objectives—quarterly, mid-year, and year-end. Ask what you can do to help achieve those goals. A legitimate concern for your boss and his goals helps build trust. Your boss should begin to perceive you as a resourceful and valuable employee.

Sample questions:

- *"What are your business priorities?"*
- *"How can I help you get your job done?"*
- *"What can I take off your plate?"*
- *"What things drive you crazy?"*

Go a step further and find out who your boss reports to, then find out that person's goals. You can do this by asking non-threatening questions like, "What are the goals you have established with your boss?" "How can I help you achieve those goals?"

Corporate Goals

Understand the company's vision and mission. Vision and mission statements are corporate philosophies and goals that companies spend a lot of time and money developing. Also, read the posters on the walls, read the Annual Report, read the corporate Home Page on the Internet, read the news releases with direct quotes from executives. Whatever you do know and be prepared to discuss the company's vision.

Realize that gathering most of this information will take some time. Don't feel panicked that you have to collect everything on your first day. But as time goes on, you'll want to be familiar with the way the company operates, who holds what positions, where the players are trying to take the company, and what the company's overall mission is.

Role of Teammates

Being perceived as a team player is key. Find out who your teammates are, get an idea of each individual's role on the team—where their performance is ranked, how the boss perceives them, what specific contributions they make outside of their job description.

Work with your teammates to help them meet your boss's overall goals. Respect others' roles, objectives, and strengths. Learn from them. Grow from them.

Sports Talk—Find out who your best three-point shooter is, know who scores at the buzzer.

Company Organizational Chart

Get a copy of the organization chart—department, division, company-wide. You'll want to review the organizational chart with your boss. Understanding how your department, division, and company are laid out is key to knowing what relationships you'll want to cultivate for future opportunities. Review with your boss each department's function and objective.

While you're at it, set out to uncover the real players in the organization, the decision-makers. For example, ask your boss who approves travel expenses, new equipment and technology purchases, and budgets for the department, the division, and the company as a whole.

Once you've established a good relationship with your boss's secretary and other people on the team, you might also listen to find out the areas and people elsewhere within the company your boss is having trouble with. For example, the finance manager might challenge your boss's efforts to approve travel vouchers. It might be best not to sing the praises of someone your boss doesn't necessarily get along well with.

Sports Talk—*Know the team captain, the head-coach, and the owner. Find out who's really calling the plays with one second to go in regulation.*

Policies and Procedures

Many companies require you to sign a company code of business conduct. Read it carefully (it will include justifiable reasons for terminating you), and abide by the code.

Outside of the code of business conduct, you should receive a handbook or binder detailing general policies and procedures. If you don't have these resources, get them from Personnel. Review policies with your boss—old, new, and recently changed.

30-60-90 Day Action Plan

To meet your specified targets and objectives, get in the habit of using an Action Plan. An Action Plan is simply a detailed list of activities you need to complete in order to move on to the next step in meeting your goals. An Action Plan gives a clear direction and purpose to your activities. Think of it as a glamorized goal setting document with a different name.

To put together an Action Plan, you'll need to know your goals and objectives (*see how asking all those questions about your job description comes in handy?*). Understand your specific targets from the first meeting with your boss. You can then begin to spell out the tasks you need to accomplish to get to your goal.

Let's go back to the example of 50 phone calls a day. You might decide that in order to answer 50 calls a day, you'll need to have a directory handy. You might determine that to answer calls faster, that you'll want to memorize extensions and helpful phone numbers. In order to do that you might decide to take the directory home and study for one hour each night until you memorize what you need. These activities become part of your Action Plan to achieve your goal of 50 calls a day. You can do this with every target you have. Just think of ways you can accomplish what you need and set out to do them.

Once you've completed your Action Plan, take the initiative to share it with your boss. You might ask for his input on ways to *add* to your plan. I emphasize the word add because you don't want to ask your boss to help you *create* the plan. That's just too much work to ask him to do. Rather, you want to show him you're a self-starter, and you also value his experience. It may turn out that he has a tool, a form, or an activity tracker that he uses and would like to share with you. If he doesn't, make up your own or use the one at the end of this section.

Review and update your Action Plan monthly. Transfer incomplete items to the next set time frame in your Action Plan. This will help you stay on track to meeting your goals.

Use the following Action Plan form to get started. And don't forget to reward yourself when you reach significant accomplishments!

Action Plan

Date: _____

Overall Goal:

_____

_____

_____

Current Situation

_____

_____

_____

30 Days

Priority	Activity	Target Date	Actual Date
_____	_____	_____	_____
_____	_____	_____	_____
_____	_____	_____	_____

60 Days

Priority	Activity	Target Date	Actual Date
_____	_____	_____	_____
_____	_____	_____	_____
_____	_____	_____	_____

90 Days

Priority	Activity	Target Date	Actual Date
_____	_____	_____	_____
_____	_____	_____	_____
_____	_____	_____	_____

What do I need to accomplish my goal?

_____

_____

_____

What resources do I need?

_____

_____

_____

Appendix 6 | Performance Appraisal Processes

Performance Management

This method is designed to more completely monitor performance, goal setting, and coaching sessions. Performance Management focuses on employee development. Team members, peers or even customers may assess performance as well as the manager.

The goal: To encourage managers and employees to share responsibility for making sure they understand the business objectives and for evaluating employee performance. Feedback is ongoing and performance reviews are more frequent than with other processes.

360-degree Feedback

As organizations change and management structures become flatter, an increasing number of companies, especially high-tech companies, are using the "360-degree Feedback" or "Full Circle" process to assess performance.

These assessments are based on feedback given from both inside and outside the company. In the case of a sales representative, the internal source could be his manager and the external source a current client or prospect. The company gains the ability to see how customers rate their sales rep. In a non-threatening way, internal and external feedback helps identify what skills need to be improved and what behaviors should be modified.

Continuous Improvement Review (CIR)

The purpose of CIR is to ensure that employees focus on quality, productivity improvements, and rewards. This assessment process rewards people for making a particular system work better. The manager and the team negotiate the percentages of system improvement and team productivity to be measured. The total review focuses on customers, the team, and the employee's contribution to system improvements. Processes are re-examined across departments and divisions. Individual and team performance is monitored over time, with a focus on correcting system problems, and not just individual deficiencies. Managers are provided with detailed records of how each person improved quality and how the system output increased—as well as how well the team performed. The data is logged so there need be no last minute collection of material.

Appendix 7 | Performance Appraisal Tracker

Performance Appraisal Tracker

_____ I met with my boss to discuss my performance appraisal.

Date: _____

_____ I know the measurement process.

Name of process: _____

_____ I've identified the elements of my performance.

Elements: _____

_____

_____

_____

_____ I've scheduled a follow-up meeting to review my Action Plan.

Date & Time: _____

_____ I've reviewed my objectives and put together my Action Plan

Appendix 8 | Asking Your Boss for Assistance

As we discussed earlier, you don't want your boss to think you're clueless, so make sure you tell him all the things you've done to get the help you need. Be specific about the type of help you need, try to be brief, let him know approximately how much time you'll need, don't overuse him, and even if you feel he failed to help you, say thanks.

Let's look at some of the types of help you might need and some possible ways to approach the task.

"Boss . . . Help! . . . Who handles such and such?"

If searching the company directory or Intranet didn't work, you could ask the company operator. If you still come up short, ask your boss. If he knows the name but not the person's number, instead of saying, "Oh, and do you have that number?" thank him for the name, and tell him you'll find the number. If he doesn't know the name, ask him who he would recommend that you ask. Thank him for his time.

"Boss . . . Help! . . . I need a second opinion . . ."

Again, we mentioned earlier the importance of not asking your boss to come up with everything you need to get your work done, but instead bringing solutions with you, or having whatever you're working on nearly complete. If you want a second opinion about your presentation, bullet-point (these are usually no longer than one sentence) the content, and ask his opinion. Does he think you need to add or remove a topic? Is it short or long enough? Then ask if he'd like you to present to him before your actual delivery. Remember to thank him for his time.

"Boss . . . Help! . . . What do I do?!*"

If you're faced with an unfamiliar task or business issue, though it might be new territory, come up with at least one solution—even if you have to get that idea from your teammates or counterparts. And though the solution may not be the one your boss recommends, it's important that he knows you're capable of facing a new task rather than running from the challenge. You'll want to ask for further "instruction" and the best way to continue approaching the task. Listen carefully, ask for clarification. Let him know you'll give him a summary of your work. Remember to thank him for his time.

"Boss . . . Help! . . . How do you work this program?"

If you're asking how to use a tool like Microsoft's Outlook Calendar or Excel there are a few things you must do *before* you go to your boss. Start by reading the user guide. Go through the software's tutorial and try to figure out as much on your own as possible. Sign up for a class. Ask a teammate who's familiar with the program if they could spend five or ten minutes to help you— not help you in general, but help you with a specific task (like showing you how to do an auto-sum calculation in Excel).

If you've exhausted your resources and done your best to understand how to work Excel, and you still have a question, and you know your boss knows how to do what you're asking, go ahead and ask him if he has a few minutes to help you.

Let's say you need help sorting information within an Excel spreadsheet. Let him know what you need and ask him what would be best. Would he like to come to your desk where the spreadsheet is open on your computer? Would he like you to email him the spreadsheet? Would he like to open a spreadsheet of his own and show you? Let him decide. If the task becomes more involved than you both anticipated let him know you'll figure the rest out. Thank him for his time. And if this type of work is an integral part of your job, you might ask if he would allow you to take the next class that's being offered (find out the details and get the information back to him for approval).

"Boss . . . Help! . . . Jill Smith hasn't called me back . . ."

After having done your absolute best several times to reach a person, let your boss know how many times you called or emailed, and ask him *what else* he thinks you should do. And, remember you're not telling him to get the other person in trouble, but to ask for another idea. So don't say the person won't return your calls, instead, say you've been unable to reach so and so.

Note: Some bosses prefer that you go to them for whatever you need. If this is so (remember you'll find this out after your initial meeting with him), find a way to comply until he expresses comfort with your doing otherwise.

Requesting Information

Take a look at the following ideas about how to request informa-tion. Let's use this scenario to show how you would request information from your co-worker group.

Scenario:

Let's say your manager asks you for a general report updating him on the status of a client issue. Let's say your boss has asked for a completed report in one week. To complete the report, you'll need information from someone in your co-worker group. How do you request this information?

Requesting Information From Your Teammates, Counterparts, Resource or Support People

To this group of people, live requests (face-to-face or over the phone) are ideal. They are more direct, and you have a better chance of getting what you need more quickly. Phone for a live conversation, or go to the person's desk.

Sample in-person conversation:

"May I interrupt you?" *Once given permission begin.* "Do you have a minute? Your assistance is needed regarding a request that's been made by my boss. My boss has asked for an update on XXX." *Saying you need a report instead of an update makes what you need from them sound time-consuming. The person may feel a lot of time is required—time they don't think they have. And you're the one who'll be putting to-gether the report anyway. So that the person you're requesting information from understands the report is your urgency and not theirs, and you could really use their involvement, tell them you have a few days to pull the information together.*

Depending on what you need, you could close with one of the following questions:

- ❑ "Would you have five minutes or so now to answer a few questions?"

- ❑ "Would you have a few minutes to give me your results?"

- ❑ "The May update outlining our client's issues was helpful. Would you mind if I made a copy of the material to include the results for my boss? When would be a good time for me to come back and pick up the originals?" *Ask if they have it in soft-copy format, and if so, say,* "If it's not too much trouble, would you take a few minutes to send May's update in an email attachment?" *Ask if they'd like you to send your request in an email. An email is generally easier for the person to be reminded of what you need.*

NOTE: If the person is overwhelmed and cannot get you what you need in the time you need it, they may recommend that you talk to someone else. That's how it is sometimes. You can then ask whomever they're recommending, but you'll want to let the first person know you're going to tell the recommended person that you were referred by them.

Voicemail
If you end up using voicemail or email rather than a live conversation, when you leave your message, you'll want to make

sure that your tone is upbeat and optimistic and conversational. By conversational, I mean at least saying that you hope they are having a good day before letting them know what you need. You could also let them know you'll be sending an email as well (in case this is the best way of reaching them, and so they'll know to be on the lookout). You can use the same content as you would in the person-to-person request.

Email

Even when you're sure email is absolutely the best way to reach the person it shouldn't be your only option. Sometimes people don't get to their emails as quickly as they respond to voicemail. Or, they may have so many to read through that yours doesn't reach their priority list when you need it to. If you don't hear back in a reasonable time, try voicemail and refer to your earlier email request. Again, if and when you do send an email, be clear and state the reason you're leaving it in the first sentence of the email message. Include any deadline you have. Use the rest of the email to explain or add details you think may be helpful. Try to limit the length of your email so it does not go beyond the opening screen size. The further down a person has to scroll to read your email, the less chance you have of it not being read at all.

Example: (Unless you've never met, it's not necessary to open with your name, title, who you work for. If you haven't met, then state those things).

"Hi,
I'm sending this email to request the list of action items that resulted from your meeting with XYZ company, regarding XXX, Friday, October 7th. If at all possible, I'll need your input no later than Thursday the Xth. I appreciate your support. Please let me know when I can expect the information.

I'm preparing a report for my boss and he's asked to have it by . . . Feel free to call me if you have questions.

Thanks for your assistance!"

[First Name]
[Contact number]

Requesting Information From Other Managers or Directors

Depending on the size of the company you work for, and the reporting structure, a director may be in the same category as a senior manager.

If they have an assistant, contact that person and let them know what you need and ask what's the best way to handle the situation. Follow their lead. If your request is not urgent, use the person's office voicemail, unless their administrative assistant tells you otherwise. If they don't have an assistant, a phone call (using their office or cellular number) is probably best. Be sure you know which number they prefer.

When you call managers or directors, you will need to be very specific about what type of information you need. This is where it helps to be clear about how they can help. Should you get them on the phone, tell them who you are (first and last name, your title, who you work for and that person's first and last name), and briefly state why you're calling.

This is an example of what you might say:

"Hi, John, this is Tommy Smith, account manager. I work for Joe Thomas, director of sales. Joe has requested an account status on XYZ company by Friday. I know you're part of the resolution team and your input would be very valuable."

Depending on what you need, choose from the following:

- ❑ "Would you have a few minutes now to share with me the outcome of your October 7th meeting with the customer?" *(the customer's first and last name and title)*

- ❑ "Would you tell me where I might find that information?"

- ❑ "Would you have a few minutes to allow me to get XYZ document so I can make a copy?"

- ❑ "If you have a soft copy, would you have the form sent to me as an email attachment?"

If the person needs time to get back to you, again, ask if they'd like you to send the request in an email. And, of course, close by saying thank you.

If Leaving a Voicemail

"Hi, John, this is Tommy Smith, account manager. I work for Joe Thomas, director of sales. Joe has requested an account status on XYZ company by this Friday. I know you're part of the resolution team. Would you contact me either by voicemail or email to let me know how best to reach you for an update on your October 7th meeting with the customer (first and last name and title)? Thanks."

Or you could choose from the previous selection.

If Sending an Email

Because managers and directors can be in so many meetings, both in and away from their offices, they usually have quicker access to voicemail (either cellular or office)—unless of course they carry and use a wireless device that allows remote access to their emails. They may have set times during the day (early morning, late afternoon, or early evening) to check email. Depending on the time factor you're working under, you may decide an email is sufficient.

Should you send an email to someone at this level, again, you'll want to identify your position, who you work for, and what you're requesting early in the message. Your name is not needed, your full name is stated in the "from" section of the email, and you'll close by leaving that information as well. Again, be brief, and consider using bullet points instead of long sentences. Include a reason why their response is important (besides the fact that your boss is asking for the information) just to let them know the request is valid.

Example:

"Hi,

I'm an account manager in the national division, and I'm on Joe Thomas's team. I'm sending this email to request an update on the meeting you had with XYZ company, Friday, October 7th. If at all possible, I'll need the following no later than Thursday the Xth:

- A list of action items
- The next meeting date
- A contact name and number for client follow-up

I appreciate your support. This information will help justify the additional support we'll be able to give

your department. Please let me know if I can be
of further assistance. I look forward to your input.
I can be reached at XXX-XXXX to answer any
questions."

Sincerely,
[First and last name]
[Title]
[Contact number]

Requesting Information From Executives

At this stage in your career you may not need to make a
request for information from anyone at this level. Requesting
information from this person is usually handled by your boss or
your boss's boss. They don't want you to overstep them, and it's
really politically incorrect anyway. If you realize that in order to
meet your boss's request you'll need information from an executive, let your boss know what you need and who you need it from.
He'll probably offer to do it, but if not ask him to contact the
person and request the information. You'll most likely be asked
to pick up the information, or be a contact for the administrative
assistant to forward the information. If you need to follow up with
anyone, then you can do that, but only upon the direction of
your boss per his contact with the executive.

If you are instructed by your boss to contact an executive,
you'll most likely be talking to that person's assistant. Again,
make sure you know exactly why you're contacting them, what
you'll be asking for, and when you're to call (unless instructed to
email, phone calls are best).

That conversation might sound something like this:

"Hi. This is Tommy Smith. Jackie (executive's
name) asked my boss (state his first and last name)
to have me call you on behalf of the project my

boss is completing for her. There's some information Jackie wants my boss to have and she said she'd leave the document with you. When is a good time for me to come by and get it?"

NOTE: If you feel uncomfortable speaking to someone at the executive level (and this is understandable for now), have your boss give you guidance as to what else to say or do.

Additionally, when requesting information from your boss you can choose from the same method as well. Just remember, he doesn't work for you, so avoid "telling" him what to do. Remember to be specific about what you need, and let him know why you need the information.

Appendix 9 | Follow Up to an Initial Request *That Hasn't Been Responded To*

To Your Co-worker Group (not including other managers or directors, executives or your boss)

The same report your boss needed you to produce in Appendix 8, you still need, yet you only have a few days to spare before missing your deadline. What do you do now?

Follow up at least a day or two *before* you actually need the information, in person, by phone, voicemail or email. State that you are following up on an earlier request (you can state the day you spoke or left a voice message or email). Ask them to let you know how best to contact them to get the information you need, or ask if they could recommend another resource. State the date by which you need the information again and if you're leaving a voicemail or email, state that you look forward to their reply.

Let's go a step further. Let's say they failed to return your voicemails or emails and, as a result, you had to turn in your report without all the information your boss requested, or worse, *you missed your deadline*. Will you respond to those people who didn't give you what you needed? And do you let your boss know who didn't do what? If you decide to say or do anything, what *are* those things? *Before* doing anything, decide *if* you're going to do anything at all.

Let's look at some typical questions and reasonable answers that will help you decide.

Q: Why do you want to respond to a person who didn't get back to you and your deadline has already passed?

Your A: Because you're angry. Because you're fed up, sick and tired of being ignored.

My A: You may be taking other people's choices and behaviors personally, viewing yourself a failure because you feel you weren't able to give a complete report, or you missed a deadline. Justifiable feelings, but not good reasons to respond. We'll go into details later.

Q: What do you want to accomplish since the deadline is already missed?

Your A: You want the other person to get in trouble so you don't. You want to show the people who didn't get you what you needed that they can't get away with ignoring you. You want to let them know two can play that game. You want them to understand that payback feels worse. Or, you simply want to get the information for future reference.

My A: All understandable feelings. None are good enough reasons to respond—except the last one, of course. And if you still need the information, maybe you can get it elsewhere. We'll go into details later.

Whether you say or do anything to the people who let you down, you still need to decide if you tell your boss. Do you tell him that the reason you didn't get him what he needed was because someone didn't give you what you needed? Do you tell him about their failure to get back to you?

Q: Why do you want to tell your boss?

Your A: You don't want to get into trouble. You don't want your boss to think you don't know how to follow directions. You think your boss already questions your abilities and you want to change his mind.

My A: First, you cannot change your boss's mind—he has to do that on his own. Second, you can be up front and let him know you did everything you could to pull together the information. You could let him know what's still outstanding and that you're still attempting to get the remaining information. You could ask him if he still wants it. We'll go into details later.

Q: What will it accomplish to tell him who didn't get you what you needed?

Your A: You need to protect yourself from taking the blame. You need to shift the blame. You need to let your boss know how bad another person is at following up. You simply want an extension on the project.

My A: If you want an extension, simply ask for one and avoid blaming another person. Let your boss know you asked for the information, and you're wondering if he can direct you to other sources. Let the other needs go.

If after all of your questions and answers you still decide to tell your boss, think about who the person is that you will be telling on. Is this your teammate, counterpart, resource or support person, another manager or director, or an executive? And what perception are you going to create in your boss's mind about that person? Is it worth it?

On to more details about what you might do when people in your co-worker group let you down and you missed your deadline.

If the person who let you down is your teammate or counterpart, you could let it go without saying anything because they will likely say something to you anyway before you say anything to them. Since you probably see them or talk with them on a frequent basis, you could wait until the next natural meeting or conversation. If they don't bring up the incident, you might jokingly say, "Now you know you weren't supposed to leave me out there by myself on that last report I needed. You know you owe me one." If it's the resource or support person, ask when they will have it, and get what you need for your files. The deal is this: you're going to need to work together for a while, so there's little use in creating a tense environment. Letting them know their input was important and you counted on it is about all you really need to do. People know when they've not given you something you asked for. Generally, they've forgotten, they couldn't find the information or they just didn't know.

If you decide to say something although you may be upset, even furious, don't use angry words in your follow-up, whether in person, over the phone, by voicemail or email. If you are really angry, try writing out your feelings on a piece of paper, being as honest as you need to be to vent, and then shred the paper. This way, you've released your frustration and it's less likely to creep into the tone of your follow-up. If you're still angry, I recommend waiting a day or two and then sending a voicemail or email instead of immediately talking face-to-face or over the phone. This gives you a chance to settle your emotions.

If you leave a voicemail, do it within the office internal voicemail system. This gives you a chance to listen to your recorded message as many times as you'd like before sending it. Listen for anger and hostility in your tone and, if you hear it, erase the message and start over as many times as you need to— then send it. If you will use email, write it, but before sending it read it aloud to someone else (outside the company). Ask them what they hear in the tone (anger, hostility, frustration, disgust). If possible, print the email draft so they can read it for themselves to see if they hear any emotions.

If you take the attitude that the reason the person didn't get back to you was because of some sort of mistake, you'll be better able to leave a voicemail or email free of emotion and blame, with instead a tone of curiosity regarding their difficulties. Try not to take the lack of response personally, such as assuming they failed you because they don't like you (even if you know they don't like you), or that they're out to get you (even if they are).

If you find yourself stating the facts about how many times you tried to contact the person, use the information not as a weapon, but to help set the "assumption" tone. Assume the person may not have had the information to give you, or didn't know the answer to your question. Most times, because people don't like to admit that they don't know something, they'll just not respond. That seems to be easier for them. You can assume they must have been on vacation and forgot to leave a voicemail message or email stating they'd be out of the office. Or assume a crisis came up that totally prevented them from getting back to you (like their system crashed, or they had problems with their voicemail, or the message may have accidentally been erased— yes, all three times!). The point here is if you work as hard as you can to let it go and not try to prove anything, you'll be better for it and so will your image. The other person knows what they did. Let them live with that. And let that be good enough for you.

Assumption and fact statements to use:

❑ *"Hmm, that's really strange that you didn't get my messages, I called Wednesday morning and Friday."*

❑ *"It's so odd that you didn't get either of those messages."*

❑ *"Oh well, why don't we discuss the information now."*

❑ *"Tell me a better way to reach you, I must have the incorrect number . . ."*

Refrain from using the follow-up voicemail or email to teach a lesson. How will you know if you're teaching a lesson? If you're thinking, "I'm just going to let him know how I feel," if you're saying to yourself, "Oh no, he's not getting away with that!" Try not to use your follow-up message to blame the person. Settle in your heart that you'll deal with the consequences of the missed deadline.

You could simply leave a follow-up voicemail and/or email that says something like: "I was not able to get your feedback in time to include your information in the report for my manager. Your input is still valuable. Would you mind forwarding me the information for future reference? Feel free to let me know how I might help. Thanks."

The following is a list of words or statements to consider avoiding when communicating to people in general.

Emotional words and statements to avoid:

• *"You were wrong for not returning my calls or messages . . ."*

• *"Do you know how much trouble you got me in?"*

- *"How come you didn't call me back?"*

Emotional behaviors to avoid:
- *Ignoring the person when you see them . . .*
- *Telling a hundred people what that person did not do for you . . .*

Angry words and statements to avoid:
- *"I called you and you never returned my calls . . ."*
- *"Didn't you get my messages?"*
- *"You said you were going to give me the information by Friday . . ."*
- *"So you don't call people back?"*
- *"The next time you need something, don't even ask me . . ."*

Blaming words and statements to avoid:
- *"If you would have . . ."*
- *"Because you didn't . . ."*
- *"You made me . . ."*
- *"You said you were going to . . ."*

Since you've missed your deadline, let this be a learning experience and a chance for you to grow. And in the future, decide to ask earlier, or ask someone else who may be more reliable. Forgive and try not to hold a grudge. You'll know if you're holding a grudge because when that same person calls you for something, you'll deliberately decide to get revenge by not returning the call or responding to the email or giving them the information they need. Whether you say it out loud or not, this is called "payback." Think about the type of person you want to be perceived as. Do you want people in the workplace to think you're an avenger? That you'll "get them" if they don't do what you want? Of course not. Don't let someone else's behavior or character determine the person you'll be.

If the situation recurs, and you feel a pattern is developing, use a non-threatening, non-blaming approach to express the importance of working together so that business gets done. You might say, "Although you weren't able to give me the information my boss needed for the last project, I wonder if you could recommend a better way for us to work together to meet our goals in the future?" Or you could say to the person, "Unfortunately, I missed you this time, what's the best way to reach you in the future?"

Remember too that with people you'll need things from regularly, whenever they ask you for something get it to them the way you would want them to get it to you. This teaches them that they can count on you, and also helps them remember that the next time you ask for their assistance, they owe you one because of how you helped them.

Another reminder: When people leave you voice messages or emails, acknowledge their message. Return the call or email in a timely fashion. Complete what's asked of you. If you get a call and it's regarding something another person handles, forward the message to the correct person, but also let the person who sent you the request know what you've done. Don't let things sit out in outer space. People have a need to know what's going on. Even if you don't have what they need, just get back to them, and say *something*. Follow up on tasks until they are complete, or until your involvement is no longer needed.

NOTE: In nearly all cases, if the person is a manager, director, or executive, you might consider saying nothing at all. Believe me, people know when they've failed to get back to you. The truth has a way of coming out, sooner or later. You might let your boss know that despite your efforts, you didn't hear back from the person. Let your boss make further contact if he feels led to do so. Otherwise, you and your boss can come up with another person to contact.

If it's your boss who hasn't gotten back to you, simply get in touch with him and, *again*, ask him for the information as if it's the first time you've ever mentioned your need (refrain from reminding him that he missed your deadline).

Appendix 10 | Disagreements

. . . are legitimate when you're disagreeing about policies and procedures that affect the ability to conduct business. The focus should not stay on who's wrong or right, but rather on how to clarify the issues that are blocking the completion of business. For example, if you're not in agreement as to which form to complete for the business of shipping out equipment to a customer, then that's a legitimate issue that needs to be clarified. You can be the person to recognize that there is an issue that needs clarification. Understand that the disagreement is not personal—you're not purposely trying to make someone else's job harder, nor are they trying to frustrate you and make your job harder. The fact is, which form to use needs to be clarified.

Disagreements are not valid and worth pursuing when resolving them is not necessary to completing business and you just don't like the way someone talked to you or their attitude. If business can be accomplished, then it might be helpful for the working relationship to try and understand what the real issue is.

Back to the form. Suppose someone disagrees over using a form that you require. You might say something like, "I had the understanding that this form has been approved. Do you mind sharing with me what about this form is making this a challenge?" Or "Help me understand. Are there areas I'm not completing that are making it more challenging?" Or, "Since this form is acceptable, and the only one I have, how might we help each other get through this so our goals are met?"

Disagreeing With Teammates, Counterparts, Resource or Support People

At the point of disagreement, at the point where business ceases to move forward, stop and remember that an issue needs to be clarified. If you're told you have the wrong form, be open to hearing which form is correct. You might say, "I understand. Could you tell me which form is correct?" If you believe you have the correct form and they don't, you could say, "Let's make sure we have the same version, mine is dated 12/1/00, what's the date on yours?" Or you could say, "According to an email I received on 12/1/00, this is the form we are to use. Do you have something more recent?" If both of you have what you believe to be right, it's even possible that you both might be. There's still no need for an argument. In a very humble tone you could say, "Seems like someone above us forgot to let us know that something has changed. Why don't we ask for clarification? Why don't we both send emails and see what is decided?"

Disagreeing With Other Managers or Directors

Let's say you're trying to offer a program that you believe is available, but a manager or director said it is not. Let's say you were told differently by your own boss, or, that the written information you were given says something different. There is clearly a disagreement. You might say, "Thank you for pointing out the change. For future reference, could you tell me where I could find written documentation of that change in policy? The latest version I have is 12/1/00." If you both have the same version, then it's possible that one or both of you have overlooked a key detail. Be open to their explanation. For example, you might say, "I'm looking at the document and I don't see the change. Could you show me what you're referring to?" And if you're obviously correct, be modest in how you point that out. You might say in a very humble tone, "Let's look at the next line. Reading that paragraph gives me the impression the policy is still in place. How do you read that?" If there is still a lack of agreement, it's a good time to agree that additional clarification is needed. Offer to look into the matter. Speak with your boss either by voicemail or by email, and copy the person you are disagreeing with on that communication.

You might send a message like this: "John and I were reading the guidelines and there's an area that needs clarification so there can be approval regarding a program I offered to our customer. Would you mind looking into this? We'd like to know your thoughts. Thanks!"

With this group of people, again, you're not trying to be right or prove them wrong you're simply working together to meet a common goal—doing business. The perception you're creating here is one of being a humble team player whose main interest is following the correct procedures for the business to run smoothly and profitably. Let people see also that you're not afraid of being corrected, nor are you afraid to ask for help. And also realize when it's time to get your manager involved. You are not to fight with people to get the job done. That is your manager's job, not yours.

NOTE: If you've been communicating via voicemail or email and suddenly a heated disagreement arises, end the voicemail or email cycle. Go to the person or pick up the phone and talk the matter over. If you do the in-person, in-the-office talk, look for an opportunity to sit down and talk face-to-face—don't stand over the person or in the doorway of their office. When invited inside as hard as it might be, as justified as you might feel, resist the urge to slam the door. Ask if it's a good time to talk and gently close the door behind you. Even though the conversation is serious, make an effort to keep a slight smile on your face, a look of hope. And keep your voice down. Again, depending on the nature of the discussion, it may be wiser to talk somewhere away from the office.

Disagreeing With Your Boss

In this circumstance, it all depends on what you're disagreeing over. Disagreements over policies, procedures and decisions he's made are not battles you should take on, unless your boss specifically asks you for your input or your personal opinion. In this case, the way you phrase your input is important. You always want to reassure the boss that you recognize he is intelligent and capable (especially if the two of you are not alone). You might say, "To build on your idea, I would offer the possibility of considering this approach." Or, "I really like your thoughts" (even though you may not agree with them). There's always the chance that your boss is trying to see what type of person you are by the way you respond—do you trust him, are you going to support him, are you loyal? So just be careful about disagreeing with your boss over decisions and policies, whether with him directly or with others in the workplace. Be careful when others ask you what you think about your boss's decisions. You must always support the boss when speaking with others, no matter what.

Let's say you really blew it and got angry and disagreed with your boss openly or challenged him on something. What do you do now? Well, an apology goes a long way especially because most people won't admit to the fact that they could have made a better decision. So recognizing an area you could have handled better is wonderful and says you're the type of person who is willing to grow. You might simply say, "I've thought about our exchange and I don't feel good about the way we interacted. I wasn't listening as intently as I would have liked, and I apologize." Or "I apologize for challenging your decision. That was not the right thing to do. Now that I've thought about it, I realize I just had a concern about how to notify my clients of the change, since I've already communicated the old procedure. What ideas do you have about how I could handle this?"

With Executives Who Set Company Policies

Again, you don't want to openly disagree with them. You want to avoid disagreeing with them, unless you've been invited to participate in a discussion and you're asked for an opinion. Even here, bring solutions and avoid simply restating problems. They *know* there are problems—that is why you're having a discussion in the first place!

When it Comes to Company Policies

Get over yourself and how great you believe all your ideas are and how you could have come up with something so much better! These people have already decided the what, the when, the how, and the why, and obviously they believe they are correct. There are just some things you will not have an input in no matter how much the corporation values employee feedback. There's always a leader who may make decisions apart from you for a reason that you may not know about or agree with. Complaining openly to others in the workplace only makes you look like a whiner. If there is a suggestion box, a roundtable discussion, a planning meeting or a forum, your opinion probably counts. If not, consider making the best of the existing decision, finding creative ways to support it even if you don't agree with it. At the least your image as a team player is being improved.

Disagreeing With Customers

In a case where a customer has been told two different things, for example, quoted two prices, well—I think we all know, the customer is always right. Nevertheless, while you always want to say things that will make the customer feel you understand and believe them, you also want to protect the company and yourself. You could listen to their complaint, do whatever research is necessary, ask for names or documentation of what they're referring to. If you cannot give the customer exactly what they're asking for after you've exhausted your resources, come up with something comparable.

If the customer is still not satisfied, you can elevate the situation or refer them to someone higher than you for resolution. Always give the person you referred them to a heads-up, either by phone or email, and briefly outline the issue and what you've done to try and resolve it. If you can resolve the issue with the customer, you'll want to let them know this is a one-time situation and not set the expectation that you're going to give them just anything they want all the time. You could say: "Because you were told one price, although the policy has since changed, I'll honor that price. But for any orders after this one, I'll have to charge the current price."

If you're in a customer-service related profession, your training is likely to include all the ways your company wishes you to handle such situations. If that information is not available, ask for it.

Appendix 11 | Recommended Reads

Account Management
Miller, Robert B., and Stephen E. Heiman, with Tad Tuleja. *Successful Large Account Management*. New York: H. Holt, 1991.

Business Etiquette
Pachter, Barbara, and Marjorie Brody, with Betsy Anderson. *Complete Business Etiquette Handbook*. Paramus, NJ: Prentice Hall, 1995.

Sabath, Ann Marie. *Business Etiquette in Brief: The Competitive Edge for Today's Professional*. Holbrook, MA: Bob Adams, Inc., 1993.

Business Tips
Boldman, Lee G., and Terrence E. Deal. *Escape From Cluelessness: An Antidote to Cynicism, Confusion, Corporate Doublespeak & Other Ailments of Today's Workplace*. New York: AMACOM, 2000.

Covey, Steven R. *The Seven Habits of Highly Effective People: Restoring the Character Ethic*. New York: Simon & Schuster, 1990.

Fox, Jeffrey J. *How to Become CEO: The Rules for Rising to the Top of Any Organization*. New York: Hyperion, 1998.

Fudzie, Vince, Andre Hayes, and the Boyz. *The Sport of Learning: A Comprehensive Survival Guide for African-American Student-Athletes*. North Hollywood, CA: Double Play Publishing Group, 1995.

Griffin, Jack, with Jill Frank, Sara Unrue Koulen, and Susan M. Osborn, Ph.D. *The Unofficial Guide to Climbing the Corporate Ladder*. Foster City, CA: IDG Books Worldwide, Inc., 1999.

Ireland, Karin. *The Job Survival Instruction Book: 400-plus Tips, Tricks and Techniques to Stay Employed*. Second Edition. Franklin Lakes, NJ: Career Press, 1996.

Maxwell, John C. *The Winning Attitude: Your Key to Personal Success*. Nashville, TN: Thomas Nelson, 1993.

Nelson, Bob. *1001 Ways to Take Initiative at Work*. New York: Workman Publishing, 1999.

Pardoe, Blaine Lee. *Cubicle Warfare: Self Defense Strategies for Today's Hypercompetitive Workplace*. Rocklin, CA: Prima Publishing, 1997.

Peters, Tom, and Nancy Austin. *A Passion for Excellence: The Leadership Difference*. New York: Time Warner Books, 1985.

Pitino, Rick, with Bill Reynolds. *Success Is a Choice: Ten Steps to Overachieving in Business & Life*. New York: Broadway Books, 1997.

Randall, Karen. *The Twelve Truths About Surviving and Succeeding in the Office—And Some of Them Aren't Very Nice*. New York: The Berkeley Publishing Group, 1997.

Riley, Pat. *The Winner Within: A Life Plan for Team Players.* New York: Putnam's Sons, 1993.

Shanahan, Mike, with Aaron Schefter. *Think Like a Champion: Building One Victory at a Time.* New York: HarperCollins, 1999.

Stiegele, Robert F. *Never Read a Newspaper at Your Desk: The Fundamental Principles of Business.* New York: Carol Publishing Group, 1994.

Toms, Michael, and Justine Willis Toms. *True Work: Doing What You Love and Loving What You Do.* New York: Bell Tower, 1998.

Tracy, Brian. *The 100 Absolutely Unbreakable Laws of Business Success.* San Francisco: Berrett-Koehler, 2000.

Watson, Charles E. Ph.D. *What Smart People Do When Dumb Things Happen at Work: Hundreds of Tips for Dealing With the Blunders, Glitches, Traps and Setbacks That Sabotage Your Road to Success.* Franklin Lakes, NJ: Career Press, 1999.

Career Advice

Peters, Tom. *Reinventing Work: The Brand You 50.* New York: Alfred A. Knopf, Inc., 1999.

Simonsen, Peggy. *Career Compass: Navigating Your Career Strategically in the New Century.* Palo Alto, CA: Davies Black Publishing, 2000.

Communication

Ferrara, Cosmo F., Ed.D. *Writing on the Job: Quick, Practical Solutions to All Your Business Writing Problems.* Englewood Cliffs, NJ: Prentice Hall, 1995.

Strugeon, Linda Braxton, and Anne Russell Hagler. *Personal Letters That Mean Business*. Englewood Cliffs, NJ: Prentice Hall, 1991.

Dress

Bixler, Susan, and Nancy Nix-Rice. *The New Professional Image: From Business Casual to the Ultimate Power Look—How to Tailor Your Appearance for Success in Today's Workplace*. Holbrook, MA: Adams Media Corporation, 1997.

Repinski, Karen. *The Complete Idiot's Guide to Successful Dressing*. New York: Alpha Books, 1999.

Seitz, Victoria A. *Your Executive Image: How to Look Your Best & Project Success—For Men & Women*. Holbrook, MA: Adams Media Corporation, 2000.

Lessons Learned

Edler, Richard. *If I Knew Then What I Know Now: CEO's and Other Smart Executives Share Wisdom They Wish They'd Been Told 25 Years Ago*. New York: The Berkeley Publishing Company, 1995.

Managing Emotions

Weisinger, Hendrie. Ph.D. *Anger At Work*. New York: Morrow/Avon, 1995.

Weisinger, Hendrie. Ph.D. *Emotional Intelligence at Work*. San Francisco: Jossey—Bass, 1998.

Mentors

Wickman, Floyd, and Terri Sjodin. *Mentoring: The Most Obvious Yet Overlooked Key to Achieving More in Life Than You Dreamed Possible. A Success Guide for Mentors & Proteges*. New York: McGraw-Hill, 1997.

Miscellaneous

Levine, John R, Carol Baroudi, and Margaret Levine Young. *The Internet for Dummies*. Foster City, CA: IDG Books Worldwide, 2000.

Motivational/Personal Development

Covey, Steven R. *First Things First: To Live, To Love, To Learn, To Leave a Legacy*. New York: Simon & Schuster, 1994.

English, Martin. *How to Feel Great About Yourself and Your Life*. New York: McGraw-Hill, 1999.

Loyd, Sam R. *Developing Positive Assertiveness*. Menlo Park, CA: Crisp Publications, 1995.

McNally, David. *Even Eagles Need a Push: Learning to Soar in a Changing World*. New York: Dell Publishing, 1994.

Ziglar, Zig. *See You at the Top*. Gretna, Louisiana: Pelican Publishing Company, 1998.

Networking/Socializing

Burley-Allen, Madelyn. *Listening: The Forgotten Skill*. New York: John Wiley & Sons, 1995.

Harkins, Phil. *Powerful Conversations: How High Impact Leaders Communicate*. New York: McGraw-Hill, 1999.

Martinet, Jeanne. *The Art of Mingling: Easy, Fun and Proven Techniques for Mastering Any Room*. New York: St. Martin's Press, 1992.

Roane, Susan. *How to Work a Room: Learn the Strategies of Savvy Socializing—For Business and Personal Success*. New York: Warner Books, 1988.

Performance Appraisals

Edwards, Mark R., and Ann J. Ewen. *360 Degree Feedback: The Powerful New Model for Employee Assessment & Performance Improvement*. New York: AMACOM, 1996.

Grote, Dick. *The Corporate Guide to Performance Appraisals*. New York: AMACOM, 1996.

Sales Techniques

Anderson, Kristin, and Ron Zemke. *Delivering Knock-Your-Socks-Off Service*. Second Edition. New York: AMACOM, 1998.

Heiman, Stephen E, and Diane Sanchez, with Tad Tuleja. *The New Strategic Selling: The Unique Sales System Proven Successful by the World's Best Companies*. New York: Warner Books, 1998.

Jellison, Jerald M. *Overcoming Resistance: Customer Relations*. New York: Simon & Schuster, 1993.

Naumann, Earl. *Creating Customer Value*. Cincinnati, OH: Thomson Executive Press, 1995.

Rackham, Neil. *SPIN Selling*. New York: McGraw-Hill, 1988.

Rackham, Neil. *The SPIN Selling Fieldbook: Practical Tools, Methods, Exercises, and Resources*. New York: McGraw-Hill, 1996.

Schiffman, Steve. *Cold Calling Techniques*. Holbrook, MA: Adams Media Corporation, 1999.

Sewell, Carl, and Paul Brown. *Customers for Life: How to Turn That One-time Buyer Into a Lifetime Customer*. New York: Doubleday, 1990.

Stewart, John. *Bridges Not Walls*. New York: McGraw-Hill, 1994.

Tracy, Brian. *Advanced Selling Strategies*. New York: Simon & Schuster, 1996.

Teamwork
Woods, John A. *10-Minute Guide to Teams & Teamwork*. Indianapolis, IN: MacMillan General Reference, 1997.

Time Management
Eisenberg, Ronni, with Kate Kelly. *Organize Your Office: Simple Routines for Managing Your Work Space*. New York: Hyperion, 1994.

Griessman, B. Eugene. *Time Tactics of Very Successful People: How to Find the Time to Accomplish the Things You Want*. Boulder, CO: CareerTrack Publications, 1995.

Lakein, Alan. *How to Get Control of Your Time and Life*. New York: P.H. Wyden, 1973.

LeBoeuf, Michael, Ph.D. *Working Smart: How to Accomplish More in Half the Time*. New York: Warner Books, 1993.

Loehr, James E. *Stress for Success: Jim Loehr's Program for Transforming Stress into Positive Energy at Work*. New York: Times Business, 1997.

Mayer, Jeffrey J. *If You Haven't Got the Time to Do It Right—When Will You Find the Time to do It Over?* New York: Simon & Schuster, 1990.

Mayer, Jeffrey J. *Time Management for Dummies*. Second Edition. Foster City, CA: IDG Books Worldwide, 1999.

Weiss, Lynn, Ph.D. *ADD on the Job: Making Your ADD Work for You*. Dallas, TX: Taylor Publishing Company, 1996.

Work Relationships/Boss Relationships
Brinkman, Rick, and Rick Kirschner. *Dealing With People You Can't Stand: How to Bring Out the Best in People at Their Worst*. New York: McGraw-Hill, 1994.

Fritz, Roger, and Kristie Kennard. *How to Manage Your Boss*. Hawthorne, NJ: Career Press, 1994.

Scott, Gini Graham. *Work With Me! Resolving Everyday Conflict in Your Organization*. Palo Alto, CA: Davies Black Publishing, 2000.

Solomon, Muriel. *Working With Difficult People*. Englewood Cliffs, NJ: Prentice Hall, 1990.

Wall, Bob. *Working Relationships: The Simple Truth About Getting Along With Foes & Friends at Work*. Palo Alto, CA: Davies Black Publishing, 1999.

Weinstein, Bob. *I Hate My Boss! How to Survive & Get Ahead When Your Boss Is a Tyrant, Control Freak, or Just Plain Nuts!* New York: McGraw-Hill, 1998.

Appendix 12 | Recommended Internet Sites

Job Search/ Job Skills/Career Guidance:

www.corporateinformation.com
Research on public, private, foreign, and domestic companies.

www.fastcompany.com/career/atoz.html
Web-based index of organizations that have been featured in Fast Company magazine.

http://www.usatoday.com/careers/careers.htm
Job seeker information, career-related news, questions and answers, career counseling.

www.vault.com
Industry information, career topic discussions, job seeker information, professional training information, and career store (for purchase of books and magazines).

http://www.acinet.org/acinet/explore.htm
Career exploration and site navigation tool—links to job skill information and services to get a job.

http://careers.wsj.com
Career journal from *The Wall Street Journal*. Job seeker information, career questions and answers, online career counseling.

www.rileyguide.com
Employment opportunity and job resources, networking, interviewing, negotiating, and employer research.

www.jobstar.org
California job search guide.

Careers & Personality Assessments:
www.self-directed-search.com
Job search and career counseling.

www.keirsey.com
Personality and temperament assessment.

www.careerdiscovery.com
Career assessment, personal career counseling and coaching.

Workplace Issues:
www.fastcompany.com
An online business magazine—focused on how companies change and compete.

Search Engines:

http://infoseek.go.com

www.lycos.com

www.webcrawler.com

www.altavista.com

www.hotbot.com

http://search.cnet.com

www.snap.com

www.yahoo.com

www.excite.com

References

Forward Foreword

Bell, Janet Cheatham. *The Soul of Success: Inspiring Quotations for Entrepreneurs*. New York: John Wiley & Sons, Inc., 1997.

Copage, Eric V. *Black Pearls: Daily Meditations, Affirmations, and Inspirations for African-Americans*. New York: Quill William Morrow, 1993.

Vanzant, Iyanla. *Acts of Faith: Daily Meditations for People of Color*. New York: Simon & Schuster, 1993.

Pre-Season | Before You Begin, Think

Geoffrey Brewer. "Brain Power." *Sales & Marketing Management*, May 1997.

Pre-Season | Before You Leave the House, Check the Mirror and the Closet

Bixler, Susan, and Nancy Nix-Rice. *The New Professional Image: From Business Casual to the Ultimate Power Look—How to Tailor Your Appearance for Success in Today's Workplace*. Holbrook, MA: Adams Media Corporation, 1997.

"Casual Dress Makes an Office Fashion Statement." Report of survey done by Evans Research Associates. *Electric Perspectives*, March-April 1996.

Fertig, Judith. "Casual Dress." *Ingram's*, August 1995.

Gitomer, Jeffrey. "Dressed to Kill at Your Sales Presentations." *Washington Post*, March 14, 1997.

Hayes, Cassandra. "How to Dress When Moving Up the Ladder." *Black Enterprise*, October 1996.

Phaneuf, Anne M. "Decoding Dress Codes." *Sales & Marketing Management*, September 1995.

Puente, Maria. "Casual Clothes Hit a Few Nerves." *USA Today: Life*, September 7, 1999.

1Q | Before You Play, Check In

Adler, Jerry. "When Email Bites Back." *NewsWeek*, November 1998.

Harrow, Robert P. Jr. "They Have Their Eyes on You: Employers Are Quietly Tracking Workers' Computer Use." *Washington Post*, November 16, 1998.

2Q | Before You Burn, Stoke Your Fire

Gaines, Lynne. "The Question Your Employees Are Afraid to Ask." *Executive Female*, September-October 1994.

Marelich, William D. "Can We Be Friends?" *HR Focus*, August 1996.

National Research Bureau. "How to Improve Your Relations With the Boss." *Supervision*, July 1996.

Halftime, Performance Appraisals & Appendix #6

Antonioni, David. "Designing an Effective 360-Degree Appraisal Feedback Process." *Organizational Dynamics*, Autumn 1996.

Grote, Dick. "Getting the Most Out of the Review Process." *HR Focus*, January 1997.

Gruner, Stephanie. "Feedback From Everyone: Are 360-Degree Performance Reviews a Silly Fad—Or a Smart Management Tool?" *Inc. Magazine*, February 1997.

Lee, Chris. "Performance Appraisals: Can We 'Manage' Away the Curse?" *Training*, May 1996.

Snader, Jack. "How Sales Reps Make 360-Degree Turnaround." *Marketing News*, February 17, 1997.

Tudor, Thomas R., Robert Trumble, and Lamont A. Flowers. "Performance Appraisals and Pay-for-Performance Plans." *Journal of Compensation and Benefits*, November-December 1996.

Weaver, W. Timothy. "Linking Performance Reviews to Productivity and Quality." *HR Magazine*, November 1996.

Off-Season | Before It's All Over, It Begins Again

Heimann, Beverly, and Khushwant K.S. Pittenger. "The Impact of Formal Mentorship on Socialization and Commitment of Newcomers." *Journal of Managerial Issues*, Spring 1996.

McGinn, Daniel, and John McCormick. "Your Next Job." *Newsweek*, February 1, 1999.

Appendix #1

Balkaran, Lal. "Corporate Culture." *Internal Auditor*, August 1995.

Goffee, Rob, and Gareth Jones. "What Holds the Modern Company Together?" *Harvard Business Review*, November-December 1996.

Robie, Richard S. "Is this Management Culture a Crocodile or Dinosaur? Don't Mistake Change for Progress." *Plant Engineering*, September 1996.

Simmonds, Linda C. "Organizational Culture." *Mortgage Banking*, June 1996.

Appendix #3

Blair, Gary Ryan. *What Are Your Goals: Powerful Questions to Discover What You Want Out of Life*. New York: Blair Publishing House, 1988.

From the Coaching Staff|Business Advice

Bell, Janet Cheatham. *The Soul of Success: Inspiring Quotations for Entrepreneurs*. New York: John Wiley & Sons, Inc., 1997.

Copage, Eric V. *Black Pearls: Daily Meditations, Affirmations, and Inspirations for African-Americans*. New York: Quill William Morrow, 1993.

Vanzant, Iyanla. *Acts of Faith: Daily Meditations for People of Color*. New York: Simon & Schuster, 1993.

Acknowledgements

My Precious Family & Friends Who
> —stayed on the phone with me *long distance* encouraging me to keep at it;
> —passed on ideas, web addresses, and book titles to help me transform my obsession about "workplace do's and don'ts" into these two books.

Mom Thank You For
> —reminding me that I had a place to come if I couldn't pay the mortgage;
> —the second payment to my editor.

Thank You Jesus For
> —not giving up on me each time I gave up on myself;
> —Your grace that influenced so many people to offer help at every turn;
> —blessing the following artists with their "good and perfect gift from above"

. . . *Patti LaBelle*—every note sounds like an original.
. . . *Roberta Flack*—you make the most painful experiences beautiful songs.
. . . *Dianne Reeves*—do you sometimes just stand next to yourself and say, "Um, Um, Um?"
. . . *Yolanda Adams*—*Mountain High, Valley Low*—every song helped me get up off the floor.

And Thank You
—Ms. Danita—for suggesting I had *two* books!
—Dr. Brewer— for time *well* spent!

To My Editors
—Connie Green, Marc DeFrancis & my "unofficial"
    editors—thanks for making me think!

To order *The Game—Winning Moves for the Male New Hire in Corporate America* AND/OR , *If Cubicles Could Talk—Conversation for the Female New Hire in Corporate America* (paperback, hardback, or electronic download) **choose from several options.**

1. Directly from Xlibris Publishers:

> Xlibris Online Bookstore
> *www.xlibris.com/thegame.html*

> Xlibris By Phone
> 1-888-795-4274 or (215) 923-4686

> Xlibris By Fax
> (215) 923-4685

> Xlibris By Email
> *Orders@xlibris.com*

2. Other Online Bookstores:
> *www.amazon.com*
> *www.bn.com*
> *www.borders.com*

3. From your local bookstore . . .

> **To contact Kim Beamon to speak at your college or special event, visit:** *www.xlibris.com/kimbeamon.html*
> **Click "Contact the Author"**